P RAYERS
Finest

*Du'a from
the Holy Qur'ân*

Mansur Ahmad

Holy Qur'ân Publishing Project
COLUMBUS, OH - ROSEMOUNT, MN

To my father,
For his teachings, and untiring effort in spreading the Truth.

Cover & Interior Design: Holy Qur'ân Publishing Project

Printed in the United States of America.
Bang Printing, Brainerd, MN.

Library of Congress Control Number 2003101720
ISBN 0-9678304-1-9

PREFACE

People have always prayed to ALLAH, whether they call Him by ALLAH, God, *Ishwar* or Yahweh. Most of the time men have worded their prayers in their own languages. ALLAH never said that He would not respond to prayers made in any language. However, the finest of the prayers are the ones worded by ALLAH Himself and mentioned in the Holy Qur'ân.

The purpose of this book is to compile such divine prayers, explain the background of revelation and the stress on the importance of such prayers in our daily lives.

Not all the supplications in the Qur'ân are included in this book. A limited discretion was used to select the prayers that would be useful in our daily lives.

I have put the words ALLAH and RABB in small caps, to remind the readers to add appropriate qualifications after the names of our RABB. For ease of reading, I have not put the words Allah subhan wa–taala or Rabbul alamin.

I would like to thank my father, Dr. Zohurul Hoque, for his inspiration and help with the transliteration. My brother Husain Nuri and his wife Shamim edited several versions of the manuscript. I am grateful to my wife Rejia for her constant inspiration. Our daugher Shabnam, a budding writer, and son Osman kept me alert on my desk. My friend Shahid Islam encouraged me with intense discussions.

If you notice any error, please inform the publisher so that the error can be corrected in the next edition, insha-ALLAH. May ALLAH distance me from such errors.

Rabbanâ taqabbal minnâ. Innaka anta-s samî'u-l 'alîm. Our Rabb accept from us. You indeed, You are the all-Hearing, the all-Knowing.

Mansur Ahmad.

Eid-ul-Adha
February 11, 2003
Rosemount, MN

PRAYER: OUR BEST STRATEGY FOR SUCCESS

A prayer or a *du'a* is not the crutch of the weak or the incapable. It is the finest strategy for all kinds of success—whether material or spiritual. For our every work, we have the option to seek help from most Knowledgeable, most Powerful resource. If such an extraordinary service is offered free of cost, should we simply ignore it? Any corporate business will jump into the best consultancy even if it requires enormous amount of money. Justice of ALLAH freely allows such consultancy, guidance, and help.

Prophets and their followers availed tremendous help by invoking *du'a*. Let such guaranteed prayers from the Qur'ân be our source of inspiration and guidance. Guidelines for successful pleading are simple: a humble heart and complete reliance on ALLAH. We must not jeopardize our prospect by inviting false divinity to help us—there is no divinity except ALLAH. Every prayer must instill in us the understanding that we by ourselves are hardly capable of doing anything; we cannot even create the air that we constantly need to survive.

Our RABB is with us every moment, whether we are awake or asleep. His constant presence ensures our safety and success. He is most Capable but we often fail to seek His help. One simple request can earn abundant help from Him. It is fascinating that the fulfillment of the request does not warrant piety. A pious is blessed, no doubt. However, a sinner can successfully invoke his RABB (*Yunus* 10:22). Even those who reject the RABB, can also be successful in reaching the RABB (*Al-A'raf* 7:190, *Yunus* 10:12). The contract between ALLAH and human is bilateral. We may unilaterally break the covenant, but ALLAH does not break His promise. He is the Provider; therefore, He provides even the sinners and unbelievers. That is the Majesty of ALLAH, which we must not underestimate.

A *du'a* from the Qur'ân is an application form already filled by ALLAH Himself, and awaits our signature. Such an application cannot fail at ALLAH's court.

Surely, when we pray, ALLAH responds.

Let us not underestimate the Power of ALLAH. He can, and He does.

For guidance in the Right Path

اَلْحَمْدُ لِلّٰهِ رَبِّ الْعٰلَمِيْنَ ۞ الرَّحْمٰنِ الرَّحِيْمِ ۞ مٰلِكِ يَوْمِ الدِّيْنِ ۞ اِيَّاكَ نَعْبُدُ وَاِيَّاكَ نَسْتَعِيْنُ ۞ اِهْدِنَا الصِّرَاطَ الْمُسْتَقِيْمَ ۞ صِرَاطَ الَّذِيْنَ اَنْعَمْتَ عَلَيْهِمْ ۙ غَيْرِ الْمَغْضُوْبِ عَلَيْهِمْ وَلَا الضَّآلِّيْنَ ۞

Al-hamdu li-llâhi rabbi-l 'âlamîn. Ar-rahmâni-r rahîm. Mâliki yawmi-d dîn. Iyyâka na'budu wa iyyâka nasta'în. Ihdina-s sirâta-l mustaqîm. Sirâta-l ladhîna an'amta 'alaihim, ghairi-l maghdûbi 'alaihim wa la-d dâllîn. [Âmîn.]

THE Hamd belong to ALLAH, the RABB of all the worlds; the Rahman, the Rahim; Malik of the Day of Requital. You alone we do serve, and to You alone we beseech for help. Guide us on the Right Path,— the path of those upon whom You have bestowed favors; not of those upon whom wrath is brought down, nor of those gone-astray. (Al-Fatihah 1:1-7)

The Holy Qur'ân begins with a salient prayer: Surah *Al-Fatihah.* Every day, we recite the *oft-repeated seven verses* (*Al-Hijr* 15:87) in our Salat. As *Umm al-Kitab,* it reflects the core values of the Holy Qur'ân. As *As-Shifa,* it cures the spiritual and social malaise.

The prayer opens with a praise to ALLAH, who is the RABB or the Lord of the Universe. The word RABB conveys not only the meaning of Provider, Sustainer, Rewarder, Ruler, Maintainer, but also nurturing, regulating, completing, accomplishing, sustaining. He is the RAHMAN—the Provider of sustenance for His creation; and the RAHIM—Most Rewarding for our activities. He is the MALIK, i.e., Master of Judgment for our good and bad deeds.

When we worship and serve ALLAH alone, we liberate ourselves from social bondage. We no more remain slaves to others, as ALLAH fulfills our all needs. We follow the path of life where ALLAH's blessings are showered. As we tread this path, we must not crush other people's rights—as Pharaoh and many evil communities did. ALLAH's wrath came to them. We must not go astray by loosing the status of Best of Creations—*Ashraful Makhluqat*—by becoming slaves to false deities or to other human's whims.

For guidance in the Right Path

وَبَنَآ ءَامَنَّا فَٱكْتُبْنَا مَعَ ٱلشَّـٰهِدِينَ ۞ وَمَالَنَا لَا نُؤْمِنُ بِٱللَّهِ وَمَا جَآءَنَا مِنَ ٱلْحَقِّ
وَنَطْمَعُ أَن يُدْخِلَنَا رَبُّنَا مَعَ ٱلْقَوْمِ ٱلصَّـٰلِحِينَ ۞

Rabbanâ âmannâ fa-ktubnâ ma'a-sh shâhidîn. Wa mâ
lanâ lâ nu'minu bi-llâhi wa mâ jâa'nâ mina-l haqqi, wa
natma'u an-yudkhilanâ rabbunâ ma'a-l qawmi-s sâlihîn.

*Our RABB! we believe, so write us down among the witnesses. And
what have we that we should not believe in ALLAH and what has come
to us of the Truth, while we long that our RABB may include us among
the righteous people?* (Al-Ma'idah 5:83-84)

Belief in the Truth leads us to a rightful life. As we vividly
witness the Truth, there is absolutely no reason to reject it. Right
Path, being sharply distinct from the wrong (*Al-Baqarah* 2:256),
guides us to the Truth. In accepting the guidance, we must not
cultivate blind faith, but promote faith on the Unseen. ALLAH
provided us with abundant intelligence. He encourages us to
use our reasoning extensively. A blind will stumble, while the
faithful uses all his faculties to reach his destination.

Early Muslims had learned the message of Truth directly
from our Rasul[PBUH]. Overjoyed with the guidance and with tears
in their eyes (*Al-Ma'idah* 5:83), they invoked this supplication.
This pivotal supplication earns for the believer a reward of
Gardens beneath which flow the rivers (*Al-Ma'idah* 5:85). In the same
verse, ALLAH reiterates that *such is the reward of the doers of good.*

*...the Right Path has indeed been
made distinct from the wrong...*

(Al-Baqarah 2:256)

For guidance in the Right Path

رَبَّنَآ ءَاتِنَا مِن لَّدُنكَ رَحْمَةً وَّهَيِّئْ لَنَا مِنْ أَمْرِنَا رَشَدًا ۝

Rabbanâ âtinâ min-ladunka rahmatan wa hayyi' lanâ min amrinâ rashada.

Our RABB! Give us mercy from Yourself and provide for us in our affair a right course. (Al-Kahf 18:10)

As we evolve in our faith, ALLAH separates us from worldly temptations, and enlightens us spiritually. The parable of the cave dwellers in Surah *Al-Kahf* reminds us that ALLAH can miraculously guide people in the Right Path. ALLAH is the Best of the teachers, He teaches us the Qur'ân (*Hud* 11:1, *Ar-Rahman* 55: 2, *Al-Qiyamah* 75:19) and thereby shows us the Right Path, only if we enroll to be His students.

Few youths, from the Essence of Jews, were searching for the Truth. They withdrew to a cave located in the Qumran Valley near Dead Sea, and pleaded for guidance. ALLAH listened to them and isolated them from their communion for many years. The youths continued to be faithful to their RABB as they woke up from their sleep (*Al-Kahf* 18:14). Others in the communion, who did not seek guidance, had strayed away.

When situation around us is maliciously against the Faith, this supplication insulates us from the evil and guides us towards the Right Path.

And those who belie Our Messages are
deaf and dumb in utter darkness...

(Al-An'am 6:38)

For acceptance of prayers

رَبِّ اجْعَلْنِى مُقِيمَ الصَّلَوٰةِ وَمِن ذُرِّيَّتِى ۚ رَبَّنَا وَتَقَبَّلْ دُعَآءِ ۞

Rabbi-j'alnî muqîma-s salâti wa min dhurriyyatî; rabbanâ wa taqabbal du'âi'.

My RABB! make me steadfast in Salat and from my offspring; our RABB! and accept my prayer. (Ibrahim 14:40)

One of the primary foundations of Islam is Salat. All the spiritual benefits of Salat may remain beyond our comprehension. Yet some worldly benefits are readily apparent—we become early risers, become punctual and responsible, we maintain perfect hygiene and discard racism. These are only few of the long lists of benefits. Since Salat helps us in so many ways, we must strive to perform and perfect it.

We should seek help from ALLAH in establishing Salat if we wish to see our children and ourselves as successful. Prophet Ibrahim[PBH], as the father of two sons—Isma'il and Is-haq[PBT], had similar parental desire. He pleaded to ALLAH to make him and his children steadfast in Salat. As the patriarch of believers, he thoughtfully included all of us as his progeny in this supplication. The majesty of the prayer lies here.

Our sincere Salat may help us reap all its worldly benefits; however, it remains with ALLAH to accept our Salat for our spiritual advancement. Through this supplication, we beg ALLAH not to reject our prayers. If ALLAH wills, He will reward us for our attempt in performing a Salat.

And to ALLAH belong all the finest Names,
so call upon Him by these...

(Al-A'raf 7:180)

For good in both worlds

رَبَّنَآ ءَاتِنَا فِى الدُّنْيَا حَسَنَةً وَّ فِى الْأَخِرَةِ حَسَنَةً وَّ قِنَا عَذَابَ
النَّارِ ۞

Rabbanâ âtinâ fi-d dunyâ hasanata<u>n</u> wa fi-l â<u>kh</u>irati hasanata<u>n</u> wa qinâ 'a<u>dh</u>âban nâr.

Our RABB! give us good in this world, and good in the Hereafter, and save us from the chastisement of the Fire. (Al-Baqarah 2:201)

In the rat race of life, we exert tremendous efforts for physical substances. Some times the sought-after items seem to be in short supply. Immaturely, we ask ALLAH to fulfill our worldly desires only: *our RABB! give us in this world* (Al-Baqarah 2:200). ALLAH points out that such a prayer is insufficient, as it does not address the share in the Hereafter. He guides us to encompass *hasanah* (lit. *good)* for all spheres of the life: in this earth, as well as in the Hereafter. On top of that, we should plead for protection from the Fire. When ALLAH Himself words this supplication, and then instructs us to plead with it, do we need any further stimulus? The *hasanah* from ALLAH is never in short supply; they are priceless yet waiting for our asking.

Ibn Kathir identified the *hasanah* as mercy and blessings from ALLAH. The result of following this *hasanah* from ALLAH is good for the person everywhere in this world (Al-i-'Imran 3:198; Al-Nahl 16:97). The life in itself is a positive gift from ALLAH, and as such is not to be despised. In this context, the word *hasanah* encompasses all-round satisfaction of mind that cannot be delimited by purely material or tangible riches. Throughout the Qur'ân, ALLAH assured people that reward for good is always better and bestowed in this world as well.

...By whatever you call, His are then the most beautiful names...

(Bani Isra'il 17:110)

For good in both worlds

وَاكْتُبْ لَنَا فِى هَٰذِهِ الدُّنْيَا حَسَنَةً وَّفِى الْأَخِرَةِ إِنَّا هُدْنَا إِلَيْكَ

Wa-ktub lanâ fî hâdhihi-d dunyâ hasanatan wa fi-l âkhirati innâ hudnâ ilayka.

And prescribe for us good in this world and in the Hereafter; for we are surely guided towards You. (Al-A'raf 7:156)

When Musa^{PBH} left for 40-days seclusion in the mountain, some of his followers started worshipping a calf. Upon his return from the mountain, this development shocked, saddened and angered him. He then selected 70 men of unsound faith for ALLAH's tryst, as the sin was beyond any human punishment. ALLAH gripped these apostates with an earthquake (see page 63), setting an example for the people of the future. As the earth shook, Musa^{PBH} pleaded to rescue those who were not at fault.

Similar to the previous supplication, this one also addresses *hasanah* or good in this world as well as in the Hereafter. We are not trying to name the *hasanah* in earthly terms, but leave it up to ALLAH to decide. Good for one person may not be good for another. We are aware that wealth, family, power, fame, fortune may not be good or desirable in all situations. We may find many misguided, clearly sinning people thriving in material wealth. Such material wealth alone is not true *hasanah*.

ALLAH knows best what is *good* for us—be it wealth or scanty resources, fame or humility, power or tranquility of mind, fortune or just overall happiness in the midst of financial difficulties. Likewise, He provides the best for us.

...But the clothing of reverence!—that is the best!..

(Al-A'raf 7:26)

For mercy

دَرِّبْ اغْفِرْلِى وَلِأَخِى وَ اَدْخِلْنَا فِى رَحْمَتِكَ وَاَنْتَ اَرْحَمُ الرّٰحِمِيْنَ ۝

Rabbi-ghfir lî wa li-akhî wa adkhilnâ fî rahmatika, wa anta arhamu-r râhimîn.

My RABB! protect me and my brother, and admit us to Your mercy; for You are the most Merciful of the merciful ones. (Al-A'raf 7:151)

Musa[PBH] was angry and aggrieved as some people from his community started calf worshipping. His brother Harun[PBH] was with the community although was not a participant in calf worshipping. Harun[PBH] assured his innocence to the distraught brother: he could never commit such a blasphemous act (*Al-A'raf* 7:150).

Musa[PBH] knew that ALLAH was watching the blasphemy, and he apprehended that ALLAH's wrath would be on the community. Therefore, he earnestly pleaded ALLAH to rescue the righteous from the ensuing punishment. The sin was enormous; the punishment that followed was stunning. If the sinners amend, the most Forgiving RABB promises due rewards even for them (*Al-A'raf* 7:153). Only ALLAH can see the heart, and He knows who repents after being sidetracked into apostasy. Only He knows who deserves the mercy or punishment.

As we expect, ALLAH answered the *du'a* and protected both the prophets and the true believers. ALLAH responds to every prayer, and there is no despair in His mercy.

...Call upon me, I shall respond to you...

(Al-Mu'min 40:60)

For mercy

رَبَّنَآ اٰمَنَّا فَاغْفِرْلَنَا وَارْحَمْنَا وَاَنْتَ خَيْرُالرَّحِمِيْنَ ۞

Rabbanâ âmannâ fa-ghfir lanâ wa-rhamnâ wa anta khairu-r râhimîn.

Our RABB! we believe, so protect us and have mercy on us; for You are the Best of the merciful ones. (Al-Mu'minun 23:109)

Even a cursory look at our daily acts can reveal our many mistakes. These faults and sins can be erased only if ALLAH showers His mercy.

The verses preceding and following this prayer compare and contrast the believers with the wrongdoers. The wrongdoers are destined to be of the losers if not in this world certainly in the Hereafter. As trusted bondsmen, first we are seeking protection from every evil suggestion and temptations, then we are seeking mercy on us. The protection is a forward looking desire, whereas mercy is to wipe off any and all intentional or unintentional sins committed earlier. True bondsmen will be successful by invoking ALLAH for mercy.

Our strong faith separates us from the unbelievers. Will ALLAH protect us and shed mercy on us because of our total faith on Him? Yes, if He desires. Being Merciful is one of His qualities, and definitely, He is the *Best of the merciful ones.*

...do not despair of ALLAH's mercy...

(Yusuf 12: 87)

For mercy

رَبِّ اغْفِرْ وَارْحَمْ وَأَنْتَ خَيْرُ الرَّاحِمِينَ ۝

Rabbi-ghfir wa-rham wa anta khayru-r râhimîn.

My RABB! forgive and have mercy; because You are the Best of the merciful ones. (Al-Mu'minun 23:118)

Similar to the supplication from the previous page, this supplication also pleads for forgiveness and mercy. ALLAH may forgive our sins, but unless He shows mercy on us, we may lapse into wrongdoings again. Besides, unless ALLAH shows mercy on us, we may never be admitted into the Garden. Not only are we seeking forgiveness, but also most importantly seeking mercy from the *Best of the merciful ones.*

This *du'a*, which is the concluding verse of the Surah, precedes with the words *wa qul*—'And you say'. If our Master, our RABB shows us the way to plead Him, is there any reason that we should not, or for that matter that we would be unsuccessful in such pleading?

We will be successful as ALLAH is intimately involved in our lives. He cares our joys and struggles, He listens attentively to our prayers and responds, He guides us to success, and gives us comfort when we are down. He forgives us when we know we faulted. He is there with us every moment, closer than our jugular veins. Our only effort is to ask Him for mercy. How can we not know—as qualified in this supplication—that ALLAH is the *Best of the merciful ones.*

...My mercy extends to all things...

(Al-A'raf 7:156)

13

SUPPLICATION BY MUSLIMS
For protection from hellfire

رَبَّنَا مَا خَلَقْتَ هٰذَا بَاطِلًا سُبْحٰنَكَ فَقِنَا عَذَابَ النَّارِ ۞

Rabbanâ mâ khalaqta hâdhâ bâtilan, subhânaka
faqinâ 'adhâban nâr.

*Our RABB! You have not created this in vain. Glory be to You!
therefore save us from the chastisement of the Fire.* (Al-i-'Imran 3:
191)

The Qur'ân sketches the hellfire ignited with men and stone,
an intense fire that will peel off the skin; those who enter the hell
will be smeared with pitch, boiled in water and whipped with
iron chains. The vivid, graphic description of the abode of evil
forces us to re-evaluate our deeds. There is no despair, as the
Qur'ân clearly identifies ways to avoid the hellfire.

The verse that contains this *du'a* also identifies the attributes
of the people who invoke this prayer. These Muslims perpetually
remember ALLAH, whether they are standing, sitting or lying on
their sides. This remembrance is not necessarily *zikr* or rolling
the *tasbeeh* beads. Islam does not teach remembrance of ALLAH to
be done at the cost of worldly pursuits. ALLAH has not prohibited
material wealth, instead He encourages us in the previous verse
to explore the creations, to learn the science of nature and to
research on the bounties provided by Him (*Al-i-'Imran* 3:190).
We should harvest benefits from all His creations without
exploiting any.

As we understand the Signs of ALLAH in the nature, which
is the true remembrance, we realize that all the creations has a
purpose (*Al-i-'Imran* 3:190), be it for ecological balance or for our
sustenance. From these Signs, we realize the supreme power,
creativity and thoughtfulness of our Master who is worthy of
all Praises. Therefore we invoke only Him, and none but Him,
to exercise His unquestionable supreme Authority to rescue us
from the torment of the hellfire.

For protection from hellfire

رَبَّنَآ إِنَّكَ مَن تُدْخِلِ النَّارَ فَقَدْ أَخْزَيْتَهُ ۖ وَمَا لِلظَّٰلِمِينَ مِنْ أَنصَارٍ ۞

Rabbanâ innaka man tud<u>kh</u>ili-n nâra fa-qad a<u>kh</u>zaitahu. Wa mâ li-<u>z</u> <u>z</u>âlimîna min an<u>s</u>âr.

Our RABB! surely whosoever you cause to enter the Fire, you have indeed disgraced him. And for the wrongdoers there are no helpers.
(Al-i-'Imran 3:192)

Who can be a helper on the Day of Judgment? The friends and families of the wrongdoers cannot come for their rescue. Most likely all of them, if wrongdoers themselves, will also be on an equally futile search for help. That Day, sinners will be disgraced, and the truthful will enjoy abundant help. Such help is from ALLAH, who can erase the sins if we earnestly plead and then rectify our conduct.

This and other (see pages 14, 35 and 38) prayers provide us the characteristics of Muslims who will succeed even though oppressors may torment their worldly lives. These characteristics are i) constant remembrance of the RABB, ii) concrete actions on His path, and iii) reflection on His Signs. In response to these supplications and the evidence of good conducts, ALLAH wipes off the sins and endows His servants with an entry to the Garden. Surely pious people will have honor on the Day of Judgment, a true sign of success. Disgrace is reserved for those who desired futile help from false deities and pretentious saints.

...evil is the resting place of the proud.

(Az-Zumar 39:72)

For protection from hellfire

رَبَّنَا اصْرِفْ عَنَّا عَذَابَ جَهَنَّمَ إِنَّ عَذَابَهَا كَانَ غَرَامًا ۞ إِنَّهَا سَآءَتْ مُسْتَقَرًّا وَمُقَامًا ۞

Rabbana-ṣrif 'annâ 'adhâba jahannama, inna 'adhâbahâ kâna gharâmâ. Innahâ sâa't mustaqarran wa muqâmâ.

Our RABB! turn away from us the punishment of Gehenna, its chastisement is indeed a continuous torment. Surely it is an evil place of rest and residence. (Al-Furqan 25:65-66)

Supplications are only a part of the path leading to success: actions should reflect our true nature. These actions are identified in the verses that precede and follow this prayer. Such actions include practicing humility, establishing Salat and spending moderately. We should also shun *shirk*, unjustified killing and fornication.

People who have erred, sinned or even committed *shirk*, are not in the deep pit of despair. ALLAH rescues us even from the worst possible scenario. The verses that precede and follow this supplication provide hope and a clearly charted map to reach our final destination. ALLAH forgives and rewards those who repent, believe, and consequently substitute their evil works with good deeds (*Al-Furqan* 25:63-71).

In this prayer, we remind ourselves of the punishment in the hell and admit that it is an evil place to reside. Our supplication and every action in our life therefore, are to seek protection from the chastisement of the Fire.

The Great Terror will not grieve them (–the righteous)...

(Al-Anbiya 21:103)

For protection from hellfire

رَبَّنَا وَسِعْتَ كُلَّ شَىْءٍ رَّحْمَةً وَّعِلْمًا فَاغْفِرْ لِلَّذِينَ تَابُوا وَاتَّبَعُوا سَبِيلَكَ وَقِهِمْ عَذَابَ الْجَحِيمِ ۞

Rabbanâ wasi'ta kulla shayin rahmatan wa 'ilman fa-ghfir li-lladhîna tâbû wa-ttaba'û sabîlaka wa qihim 'adhâba-l jahîm.

Our RABB! You embrace all things in mercy and knowledge. Therefore forgive those who turn, and who follow Your way, and save them from the chastisement of the fierce Fire. (Al-Mu'min 40:7)

The worst possible fate for any person would be a place in the hellfire. To protect the *ummah* from the Fire, angles and pious Muslims plead ALLAH with this verse. These angels and Muslims are recognized as the *bearer of 'the Throne of Power'* (*Arsh*)—a term indicating those who carry out the commands relating to the Power of their RABB.

This verse testifies ALLAH's love and compassion towards all creations. Even when we make mistakes, ALLAH surely knows our limitations. This supplication pleads forgiveness for those sinners who have repented, and for those who attempt to follow the right path. As ALLAH *embraces all things in mercy*, He can forgive us and protect us from the severe punishment of the hellfire.

Certainly the reverent will be in Gardens and springs.

(Al-Hijr 15:45)

For protection against *shirk*

رَبِّ اجْعَلْ هَـٰذَا الْبَلَدَ اٰمِنًا وَّاجْنُبْنِیْ وَبَنِیَّ اَنْ نَّعْبُدَ الْاَصْنَامَ ۞

Rabbi-j'al hâdha-l balada âminan wa-jnubnî wa baniyya an na'buda-l asnâm.

My RABB! make this town secure, and save me and my children from worshipping idols. (Ibrahim 14:35)

On our pleading, ALLAH forgives many sins altogether as there is no despair of His mercy (*Az-Zumar* 39:53). *Shirk* is the worst sin that is not forgiven (*An-Nisa'* 4:48,116), however if a sinner repents and amends his ways, there may be hope. Logically, we should therefore avoid worshipping idols, and avoid attributing the qualities of ALLAH to anybody, be it rulers, people in power, sheikhs, *pirs*, whether living or dead. If we shun the practice of *shirk* in any form, ALLAH showers success in our material and spiritual lives.

Ibrahim[PBH], the patriarch of monotheism, invoked ALLAH with this pivotal supplication. As a sign of highest form of well-wishing, he pleaded to save his progeny from indulging into *shirk*.

Ibrahim[PBH] also requested to protect the town of Makkah. The security of the town may connote physical protection from looting and plunder, but the best form of security is spiritual protection against invasion of *shirk*.

...You have not besides Him any patron nor an intercessor...

(As-Sajdah 32:4)

For Truth

رَبِّ احْكُم بِالْحَقِّ وَرَبُّنَا الرَّحْمَنُ الْمُسْتَعَانُ عَلَى مَاتَصِفُونَ ۝

Rabbi-hkum bil-haqq. Wa rabbuna-r rahmânu-l must'aânu 'alâ mâ tasifûn.

My RABB! You decide with truth. And our RABB is the Rahman whose help is invoked against what you attribute. (Al-Anbiya' 21: 112)

Victory rightfully belongs to the Truth. Apparent and temporary success can fool the disbelievers into thinking that they are on the right path. They thus embark on taunting as if the believers' faith had proved itself wrong. The status of our current Muslim community all over the world is not something to rejoice. In such humiliating situations, this supplication can elevate us out of our desolation. The supplication confirms ALLAH as the ultimate Judge of the Truth and that He alone protects us against blasphemies uttered by non-believers.

This supplication which is the concluding verse of Surah *Al-Anbiya'* was revealed in Makkah. Disbelievers in Makkah tortured the Prophet^{PBUH} and drove him out of his hometown. Surely, ALLAH accepted this supplication from our Rasul^{PBUH} and granted the Muslims initial success in Madinah, then in Makkah and later in Arabian Peninsula. Within a century, this success spread across the continent. Such is the far-reaching blessings of a short, but earnest *du'a.*

...ALLAH wipes out the falsehood and establishes the Truth with His words.

(As-Shuara 42:24)

For protection from evil

أَعُوذُ بِرَبِّ الْفَلَقِ ۝ مِنْ شَرِّ مَا خَلَقَ ۝ وَمِنْ شَرِّ غَاسِقٍ إِذَا وَقَبَ ۝ وَمِنْ شَرِّ النَّفَّاثَاتِ فِى الْعُقَدِ ۝ وَمِنْ شَرِّ حَاسِدٍ إِذَا حَسَدَ ۝

A'ûdhu bi-rabbi-l falaqi. Min sharri mâ khalaqa. Wa min sharri ghâsiqin idhâ waqaba. Wa min sharri-n naffâthâti fi-l 'uqadi. Wa min sharri hâsidin idhâ hasad.

I seek refuge with the RABB of the Day break,— from the evil of what He has created, namely, from the evil of the darkness when it overspreads, and from the evil of the blowers in knots, and from the evil of the envier when he envies. (Al-Falaq 113:1-5)

This and the next supplication are complete Surahs by themselves. Both the Surahs start with the word *Qul*—Say. ALLAH is commanding us to make these prayers.

Everything that is created in this earth is for our benefit, but misuse or abuse of the same results into evil. Knowledge and humility is created for us. But the darkness of ignorance and arrogance surely overpowers us. Evils of all kinds of superstition—witchcraft, charms of *pirs*, who blow into knots, water, or on the body—must be avoided at all cost. Supernatural power is the domain of ALLAH, and anybody who claims such power, or who subjects to such claims by others is a victim of evil *shirk*. We become truly free when we seek refuge with the RABB of Daybreak, who pierces all darkness and evil with the Light of Islam. We have only one Master, who is Just and does not exploit us. Such physical, moral and spiritual liberty and blessings must be the cause of envy for the evil. By enjoying the secure refuge with ALLAH, we remain immune to all kinds of envy.

...a bearer of burden cannot bear the burden of another...

(Al-Fatir 35:18)

For protection from evil

أَعُوذُ بِرَبِّ النَّاسِ ۞ مَلِكِ النَّاسِ ۞ إِلَهِ النَّاسِ ۞ مِن شَرِّ الْوَسْوَاسِ ۞ الْخَنَّاسِ ۞ الَّذِى يُوَسْوِسُ فِى صُدُورِ النَّاسِ ۞ مِنَ الْجِنَّةِ وَالنَّاسِ ۞

A'ûdhu bi-rabbi-n nâsi. Maliki-n nâsi. Ilâhi-n nâsi.
Min sharri-l waswâsi-l khannâsi. Alladhî yuwaswisu fî
sudûri-n nâsi. Mina-l jinnati wa-n nâs.

*I take refuge with the RABB of mankind, the Master of mankind, the
God of mankind, from the evil of the whispering of the sneaking one,
- who whispers into the hearts of mankind, from among the jinn or the
mankind.* (An-Nas 114:1)

This supplication, which is a complete Surah, affirms
the position of ALLAH being the RABB, Master, and God of all
creations. This Surah also starts with the command *Qul*—to
invoke this prayer.

Once we obtain refuge with the most Powerful, we can be
assured of the highest level of security. Without this security, we
become victims of evil whispering of Shaitan into our hearts.
The temptations from the jinns and men attack us in various
shapes: clear or subtle. Some times the temptations seem almost
the right path. Before we can realize, the evil ideas are imbibed
into our systems. The spread of evil is often well-designed and
supported by a network of evil jinns and men. Who can pull us
out of such quicksand other than the RABB of all Creations?

*And those who avoid the great sins and indecencies,
except minor faults—your RABB is
certainly magnanimous in forgiving...*

(An-Najm 53:32)

For protection from evil

وَقِهِمُ السَّيِّئَاتِ ۚ وَمَن تَقِ السَّيِّئَاتِ يَوْمَئِذٍ فَقَدْ رَحِمْتَهُ ۚ وَذَٰلِكَ هُوَ الْفَوْزُ الْعَظِيمُ ۞

Wa qihimu-s sayyiât. Wa man taqi-s sayyiâti yawmaîdhin fa-qad rahimtahu. Wa dhâlika huwa-l fawzu-l 'azîm.

And save them from evils. For, whomsoever You save from evils this Day, then surely You have shown mercy to him. And this indeed is the great achievement. (Al-Mu'min 40:9)

Shaitan's prime task is to deviate us by casting a strong negative influence. Resisting his evil temptation is difficult unless we get protective help from the RABB. This supplication is made by the bearer of the *'Throne of Power'*: the angels and pious Muslims who carry out all the commands of ALLAH (*Al-Mu'min* 40:7). Due to their sheer benevolence, the angels and the true Muslims pray for the whole brotherhood to rescue them from the enticement of the Shaitan.

When we plead ALLAH with these words, we are reciprocating the prayer for other Muslims. Sharing goodwill and taking care of our sisters and brothers in faith will make us a stronger community to thwart the evil designs of the Shaitan.

And if a pricking of the Shaitan pricks you, then seek refuge with ALLAH...

(Fussilat 41:36)

22

For protection from Shaitan

رَبِّ أَعُوذُ بِكَ مِنْ هَمَزَٰتِ الشَّيَٰطِينِ ۞ وَأَعُوذُ بِكَ رَبِّ أَن يَحْضُرُونِ ۞

Rabbi a'ûdhu bika min hamazâti-sh shayâtîni. Wa a'ûdhu bika rabbi an-yahdurûn.

My RABB! I take refuge with You — from the prompting of the Evil-ones; And I take refuge with You, O RABB! lest they come up to me. (Al-Mu'minun 23:97-98)

Prophet Muhammad[PBUH] was instructed to invoke this *du'a* in the face of oppression. He looked upon ALLAH as his only support, the Source of all Strength. If ALLAH provides the refuge, then the evil ones—Shaitan or the opponents from the Quraish—can do no harm. These evil forces, whatever they try, cannot inhibit the progress of Islam.

This supplication provides us courage when we are in distress and worry about attacks by the evil ones. This is an ideal supplication to be invoked everyday. Other than ALLAH, nobody has the power to rescue us when Shaitan creeps up on us. We would enjoy full protection only if we seek refuge with the most Powerful.

...Surely Shaitan is an open enemy to mankind.

(Yusuf 12:5)

23

Against oppressors

رَبَّنَآ أَخْرِجْنَا مِنْ هَٰذِهِ الْقَرْيَةِ الظَّالِمِ أَهْلُهَا وَاجْعَل لَّنَا مِن
لَّدُنكَ وَلِيًّا وَاجْعَل لَّنَا مِن لَّدُنكَ نَصِيرًا ۞

Rabbanâ akhrijnâ min hâdhihi-l qaryati-z zâlimi
ahluhâ; wa-j'al lanâ min-ladunka waliy yan, wa-j'al lanâ
min-ladunka nasîrâ.

*Our RABB! take us out of this habitat whose people are oppressors,
and make for us a protecting-friend from Your presence and make for
us a helper from Your presence.* (An-Nisa' 4:75)

Oppressors usually initiate their harassments against
economically and socially weaker people who are vulnerable
to all kinds of torture. At the same time, these weak and poor
people from the lower strung of the society are the earliest to
accept the Truth as they see the need for justice and equality.

In Makkah too, the slaves and the poorer people were
primarily targeted. Weak and oppressed males, females and
children invoked this *du'a* to ALLAH to protect them from the
oppressors. The way out of this torture was to escape to a new
location where people would be friendly. Usually escape routes
are monitored; therefore, these people invoked ALLAH for a safe
passage. At different periods, early followers of Muhammad[PBUH]
found shelter in Abyssinia and Madinah. In course of time,
these Muslims witnessed help from ALLAH to establish freedom
and peace in Makkah.

...Surely ALLAH does not love any arrogant boaster.

(Luqman 31:18)

Against oppressors

دَرَّبَّنَا اطْمِسْ عَلَى أَمْوَالِهِمْ وَاشْدُدْ عَلَى قُلُوبِهِمْ فَلَا يُؤْمِنُوا حَتَّى يَرَوُا الْعَذَابَ الْأَلِيمَ ۞

Rabbana-tmis 'alâ amwâlihim wa-shdud 'alâ qulûbihim
fa lâ yu'minû hattâ yarawu-l 'adhâba-l alim.

*Our RABB! Wipe away their wealth, and put hardness in their
hearts, it is such that they do not believe until they see the painful
punishment.* (Yunus 10:88)

The Qur'ân often cites the story of Musa^{PBH} and Pharaoh:
a clash between good and evil, and the triumph of an upright
honest man over a ruthless strong king. The king used to
command incredible power over his subjects. His monuments
continue to awestruck spectators millenniums later. His pride
and arrogance had humbled thousands. Out of these humiliated
people rose a man, not even eloquent (page 88) and a fugitive
from the ruler (page 46). This man, Musa^{PBH}, with his brother
Harun^{PBH}, had aimed to establish the rule of ALLAH in the
land of Egypt. To counter the formidable might of Pharaoh,
Musa^{PBH} resorted to a prayer: the power of which we often fail to
appreciate. Invoking prayer is hardly any sign of weakness; it is
the most prudent way to tap the abundant resources of ALLAH.
Ignoring prayer is a foolish arrogance that we cannot afford.

Every wealth belongs to ALLAH. He gives it to whom He
pleases and He takes away as He pleases. As Pharaoh misused
the wealth against the very Provider, and corrupted all the
feelings and intelligence in his heart against the principles of
ALLAH, a *painful punishment* devastated him and his empire. The
majesty of this prayer must not be underestimated, as Pharaoh
did believe in ALLAH when death overpowered him *(Yunus 10:
90)*.

Repel evil with that whichever is the best...

(Al-Mu'minun 23:96)

Against oppressors

رَبِّ ابْنِ لِي عِنْدَكَ بَيْتًا فِي الْجَنَّةِ وَنَجِّنِي مِنْ فِرْعَوْنَ وَعَمَلِهِ وَنَجِّنِي مِنَ الْقَوْمِ الظَّالِمِينَ ﴾

Rabbi-bni lî 'indaka bayta<u>n</u> fi-l jannati wa najjinî min fir'awna wa 'amalihî wa najjinî mina-l qawmi-<u>z</u> <u>z</u>âlimîn

My RABB! build for me in Your presence an abode in the Garden, and rescue me from Pharaoh and his activities, and rescue me from the oppressing community. (At-Tahrim 66:11)

Although the Qur'ân does not name the wife of the Pharaoh, she was known by her name 'Asiya. She is considered one of the four best women ever lived: the other three being Mar-yam, Khadija and Fatima. Most likely 'Asiya had rescued infant Musa[PBH] when he reached the king's palace afloat a basket.

Being the wife of a powerful man, she must have had access to every possible comfort. Her palace must have been most luxurious. Yet, she knew these earthly riches were valueless if they brought no reward in the Hereafter. She had no desire for the grandeur of royalty, but a permanent home in the Garden. Although she pleaded for the rescue from the oppressing community, most likely initially she was not a direct victim of oppression. She would be a victim only if she participated with the aggressors. Every time oppression is practiced, the oppressor earns a negative score. 'Asiya surely did not want any negatives against her. The beauty of this prayer lies in the humbleness of a queen, who is a mere slave to the King of kings.

Once 'Asiya pledged allegiance with ALLAH, Pharaoh began torturing her until she passed away. It is narrated that ALLAH had sent invisible angels who comforted her during her agony.

ALLAH is most Gentle towards His bondsmen...

(As-Shura 42:19)

Against distress

قُلِ اللَّهُمَّ مَالِكَ الْمُلْكِ تُؤْتِى الْمُلْكَ مَن تَشَآءُ وَتَنزِعُ الْمُلْكَ مِمَّن تَشَآءُ وَتُعِزُّ مَن
تَشَآءُ وَتُذِلُّ مَن تَشَآءُ بِيَدِكَ الْخَيْرُ إِنَّكَ عَلَىٰ كُلِّ شَيْءٍ قَدِيرٌ ۞ تُولِجُ الَّيْلَ فِى
النَّهَارِ وَتُولِجُ النَّهَارَ فِى الَّيْلِ وَتُخْرِجُ الْحَيَّ مِنَ الْمَيِّتِ وَتُخْرِجُ الْمَيِّتَ مِنَ الْحَيِّ
وَتَرْزُقُ مَن تَشَآءُ بِغَيْرِ حِسَابٍ ۞

Quli-llâhumma mâlika-l mulki tu'ti-l mulka man
ta<u>sh</u>âu' wa tanziu'-l mulka mimman ta<u>sh</u>âu', wa tui'zzu
man ta<u>sh</u>âu' wa tu<u>dh</u>illu man ta<u>sh</u>âu'. Bi-yadika-l
khair. Innaka 'alâ kulli <u>sh</u>ayi'<u>n</u> qadîr. Tûliju-l layla fi-n
nahâri wa tûliju-n nahâra fi-l layli, wa tu<u>kh</u>riju-l <u>h</u>ayya
mina-l mayyiti wa tu<u>kh</u>riju-l mayyita mina-l hayyi, wa
tarzuqu man ta<u>sh</u>âu' bi-<u>gh</u>ayri <u>h</u>isâb.

*Say: "O ALLAH! Master of the kingdom! You give the kingdom to
whom You please, and You snatch the kingdom from whom You please;
and You exalt whom You please and You abase whom You please. In
Your hand is all good. Surely You are Possessor of power over all things.
You cause the night to merge into the day, and You cause the day to
merge into the night; and You bring forth the living out of the dead, and
You bring forth the dead out of the living; and You give sustenance to
whom You please without reckoning!"* (Al-i-'Imran 3:26-27)

The Holy Qur'ân mentioned many supplications—some
of them were made by prophets, some by pious Muslims (not
prophets) and others were taught by ALLAH Himself. While all
these prayers are extraordinary, the ones instructed by ALLAH
are sheer magnificent.

In Surah *Al-i-'Imran*, ALLAH taught this prayer to Prophet
Muhammad[PBUH]. Commentators interpret this verse to be the
situation of the Israelites who had the kingdom, but ALLAH took
it away. From being a living nation they eventually turned into
a spiritually dead community. Arabs, who were spiritually at
the abyss, began bustling with life with the message of Islam
brought by Muhammad[PBUH]. We know that many flourishing
nations and kingdoms disintegrated. As people deviate from

the Truth, ALLAH makes them spiritually dead, politically and financially bankrupt.

When we are devastated morally, spiritually or in worldly affairs, only ALLAH can bring us back. Whether we take the *merging of day into night* literally or metaphorically, this verse shows ALLAH's majestic Power.

We are weak and insufficient, but the reward is only a prayer away. We are poor, and ALLAH distributes wealth freely as He pleases. He gives spiritual fortune to those who ask. ALLAH has improved the situations for many, and we are convinced that ALLAH will do so for us if we sincerely call upon Him.

ALLAH is the Light of the heavens and the earth.
The parable of His Light is like a light-stand, on which there is a lamp; the lamp is in a glass vessel; the glass vessel is as it were a brilliant star, it is lighted with a blessed olive-tree, neither of the East nor of the West, the oil of it well-nigh emitting light though fire does not touch it. There is Light upon Light. ALLAH guides towards His Light whom He pleases...

(An-Nur 24:35)

Against distress

آنِّى مَسَّنِىَ الضُّرُّ وَاَنْتَ اَرْحَمُ الرّٰحِمِينَ ۞

Annî massaniya-d durru wa anta arhamu-r rāhimîn.

Surely, distress has touched me, and You are the most Merciful of the merciful ones. (Al-Anbiya' 21:83)

Wealth never seemed to be an issue with Ayyub[PBH]: he had beautiful houses, plenty of livestock, granary full of grains, and a large family. ALLAH tested him by taking away all these material wealth. Things turned even worse, Ayyub[PBH] became so sick, probably with leprosy, that he was abandoned at the edge of the township. His wife supported him by working as a housemaid. During these difficult times, Ayyub[PBH] earnestly pleaded to ALLAH ascertaining his distress, but he never directly requested for the removal of the plight. He left the decision to ALLAH, but did not fail to glorify Him. It was his desire to be cured and be reestablished in life, but ultimately it is in the knowledge of ALLAH whether to grant him his wishes.

As we continue to read (*Al-Anbiya'* 21:84), ALLAH responded to the supplication, and removed the distress. Ayyub[PBH] regained his health and recovered his wealth.

During our difficult times, be it sickness, loss of job or family disharmony, this supplication is truly inspiring. We supplicate, as Ayyub[PBH] did, that ALLAH is the *most Merciful of the merciful ones.* During distress, we must continue our own insignificant effort to overcome the difficulties, while seeking that ALLAH would make our efforts easier. Indeed, ALLAH is Hearer of prayer.

and when I am sick, He then heals me;

(As-Shu'ara' 26:80)

Against distress

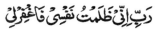

Rabbi innî zalamtu nafsî fa-ghfir lî.

My RABB! I have indeed done harm to myself, therefore You protect me. (Al-Qasas 28:16)

When we are at dark and at loss, help is only a prayer away. Here we see how a prayer rescued Musa^{PBH}. A fight had broken out between an Israelite and an Egyptian. As the Israelite cried for help, Musa^{PBH} intervened but his unintended blow killed the Egyptian. When Pharaoh came to know of this, he decided to punish Musa^{PBH} with death (*As-Shu'ara'* 26:14, *Al-Qasas* 28:20). Following this incident, Musa^{PBH} pleaded ALLAH to protect him from the consequences of an unintentional killing.

Often we forget that the protective power ultimately remains with ALLAH. When in trouble, we often solely depend on other people instead of seeking of help from ALLAH. While there is nothing wrong in seeking help from friends, families or other professionals, we should remember that help from these people could be fruitful only if ALLAH desires. In this case, Musa^{PBH} put his worldly effort by running away, although he depended on ALLAH's protection. Similarly, we must exert our own efforts in overcoming the trouble, and at the same time seek the Divine protection.

Well then! who responds to the distressed when he calls upon Him, and removes the evil...?

(An-Naml 27:62)

Against distress

رَبَّنَا اكْشِفْ عَنَّا الْعَذَابَ إِنَّا مُؤْمِنُونَ ۞

Rabbana-kshif 'anna-l 'adhâba innâ mu'minûn.

Our RABB! remove from us the punishment, surely we are Believers.
(Ad-Dukhan 44:12)

This supplication addresses people who are busy in worldly affairs and ignore ALLAH's messages. Many of us consider ourselves as true religious persons, yet become too engrossed in worldly affairs. Life will not be permanently rosy, but punishment will come in a Day with sky overcast with smoke (*Ad-Dukhan* 44:10). As punishment will befall, the rejecters will repent and will invoke this supplication. The following verse (*Ad-Dukhan* 44:13) strongly advises that we should follow the messages brought by Rasul[PBUH] before it is too late.

Although this *du'a* refers to the punishment on the Day of Judgment, we also receive punishment in this life. We can avoid the punishments by following the guidance of the Qur'ân. If we ignore ALLAH's commands, how can we expect to be pampered? Let us make *taubah* (repentance) everyday, be true believers, and invoke this supplication to remove any ensuing punishment.

*...surely We do not leave to perish
the reward of the righteous.*

(Al-A'raf 7:170)

Against distress

اَنِّى مَغْلُوبٌ فَانْتَصِرْ ۞

Annî maghlûbun fa-ntasir.
Certainly, I am overcome, so You do help. (Al-Qamar 54:10)

During oppression, who could be the best help except ALLAH? Indeed, Nuh^{PBH} had found solace in ALLAH when his community had turned against him. The community had attacked him in various ways, declaring him a madman and threatened him with death. Distraught and desperate at the opposition, Nuh^{PBH} pleaded to ALLAH by this supplication.

The Qur'ân has repeatedly asserted that ALLAH is all-Hearing, all-Seeing. He watches our every movement and He responds to our every plight. True to His promise, ALLAH responded to the pleading of His servant. The community that had raised severe opposition against the Truth now faced a deluge that mankind would dare to witness again.

As the rejecting community perished, ALLAH rescued Nuh^{PBH} even though he was sailing in a frail ship crudely built with some plank and nails (*Al-Qamar* 54:13). The Qur'ân cites this whole incident as a Sign for mankind regarding ALLAH's warning and punishment (*Al-Qamar* 54:15-16).

This supplication can be invoked if distress, danger, or defeat appears to overcome us. Surely ALLAH had answered this *du'a* in favor of Nuh^{PBH}. ALLAH's plan is best for relieving our distress.

...And they had plotted, and ALLAH planned.
And ALLAH is the Best of the planners.

(Al-Anfal 8:30)

Against distress

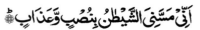

Annî massaniya-sh shaytânu bi-nusbin wa 'adhâb.
Certainly the Devil has touched me with fatigue and agony. (Sad 38:41)

In difficult times, we lose many friends and even some families. Our bases crack, and we hardly encounter the people whom we had trusted and may even had helped. The sure recourse is with ALLAH; He does not require any provisions or help from us, yet He continuously provides us sustenance. As Ayyub^{PBH} was tormented with disease and poverty, he never mistrusted his RABB. A difficulty does not mean ALLAH is inattentive: He never abandons His slaves. Ayyub^{PBH} knew that before a word comes out of his mouth, ALLAH will respond to the needs. A swift response of a motherly love turns pale in front of ALLAH's love. ALLAH provides us before our asking—be that our mundane needs or spiritual guidance.

During agony, Ayyub^{PBH} did not ask to remove his ailment. If ALLAH desires fatigue and agony for him, so be it. Therefore, Ayyub^{PBH} just stated his status. He was not in despair, as that would mean loss of faith in the protective hands of ALLAH. Surely, ALLAH responded—giving him his family and wealth *(Sad 38:43)*. Such strong perseverance made Ayyub^{PBH} *an excellent bondsman (Sad 38:44).*

...know that your wealth and your children
are indeed a temptation...

(Al-Anfal 8:28)

Against temptation

رَبِّ السِّجْنُ اَحَبُّ اِلَيَّ مِمَّا يَدْعُونَنِيّ اِلَيْهِ وَاِلَّا تَصْرِفْ عَنِّيْ كَيْدَاهُنَّ اَصْبُ اِلَيْهِنَّ وَاَكُنْ مِّنَ الْجهِلِيْنَ ۞

Rabbi-s sijnu a<u>h</u>abbu ilayya mimmâ yad'ûnanî ilayhi; wa illâ ta<u>s</u>rif 'annî kaydahunna a<u>s</u>bu ilayhinna wa aku<u>n</u> mina-l jâhilîn

My Rabb! The prison is dearer to me than that to which they invite me. And if You do not turn away their plot, I may incline towards them and become of the ignorant. (Yusuf 12:33).

As a soldier's valor is best tested in a battlefield, Yusuf's^PBH morality was tested with temptations. At one time, Aziz's wife had ineffectively seduced Yusuf^PBH. Then the ladies of the town hatched a more sinister game of enticement. This was not an infatuation, rather a vicious approach to crush the uprightness of a young slave. Aziz's wife surely wanted to humble the slave *(Yusuf* 12:32) whose morality had humiliated and embarrased her in front of her husband and others *(Yusuf* 12:25).

Though conscientious and morally stable, Yusuf^PBH worried about the collaborative strategy of the wealthy women. He knew that his moral barrier is fortified with ALLAH's blessings only. Unless ALLAH continues to support him, he personally may not be able to resist the temptation. Languishing in a jail is still preferable than being disgraced.

Although Yusuf^PBH was imprisoned, it was not a defeat for him. Rather, it was a success as the young man was able to guard his moral.

It is worth remembering that apparent loss is not necessarily a sign of punishment or rejection; a humiliating treaty at the Hudaibiyah was certainly a *Fateh Mubin*—a Clear Victory *(Al-Fath* 48:1).

Against faults

رَبَّنَآ إِنَّنَا سَمِعْنَا مُنَادِيًا يُّنَادِى لِلْإِيْمَانِ أَنْ اٰمِنُوْا بِرَبِّكُمْ فَاٰمَنَّا رَبَّنَا فَاغْفِرْ لَنَا ذُنُوْبَنَا وَكَفِّرْ عَنَّا سَيِّاٰتِنَا وَتَوَفَّنَا مَعَ الْأَبْرَارِ ۚ

Rabbanâ innanâ sami'nâ munâdiya<u>n</u> yunâdî li-l îmâni an âminū bi-rabbikum fa-âmanna; rabbanâ fa-<u>gh</u>fir lanâ <u>dh</u>unūbanâ wa kaffir 'annâ sayyiâtinâ wa tawaffanâ ma'a-l abrâr.

Our RABB! surely we have heard a Caller calling towards the Faith, saying: 'You believe in your Rabb', so we have believed. Our Rabb! protect us then against our faults, and wipe off from us our evils, and make us die with the righteous (Al-i-'Imran 3:193)

Our faults are often the cause of our sufferings. In the face of persecution, torture, and fights inflicted at us, we seek help from ALLAH to help us overcome our drawbacks. We continue to have comfort and joy realizing that ALLAH would provide us with the best reward.

When we invoke this and three more supplications from surah *Al-i-'Imran* (see pages 14, 15 and 38), ALLAH immediately responds with a reward of an entry to the Garden beneath which flows the river (*Al-i-'Imran* 3:195). ALLAH responds to these supplications made by people who perpetually remember Him during any worldly pursuits exploring all the intricacies of nature (*Al-i-'Imran* 3:191). In this *du'a* we are confirming our faith and seeking protection against faults. We are also pleading forgiveness of our sins, and seeking the bliss of a death in the state of righteousness.

...Equal are not the impure and the pure...

(Al-Ma'idah 5:100)

Against faults

رَبَّنَا اغْفِرْ لَنَا ذُنُوبَنَا وَإِسْرَافَنَا فِىٓ أَمْرِنَا وَثَبِّتْ أَقْدَامَنَا وَانْصُرْنَا عَلَى الْقَوْمِ الْكَٰفِرِينَ ۞

Rabbana-ghfir lanâ dhunûbanâ wa isrâfanâ fî amrinâ
wa thabbit aqdâmanâ wa-nsurnâ 'ala-l qawmi-l kâfirîn.

*Our RABB! protect us against our faults and our extravagance in
our affairs, and make firm our feet, and help us against the unbelieving
people.* (Al-i-'Imran 3:147)

Many times, in the face of adversity, we fail to overcome the
situation due to our weakness or faults. For Muslims, the battle
of Uhud was such a situation. Prophet Muhammad[PBUH] was so
severely injured at the battle that rumors spread that he was
dead. The battle of Uhud was the only battle where the early
Muslims suffered a set back. The fault mentioned to in the verse
refers to some of the archers who left their strategic positions on
the hillock in spite of specific orders to stick to their positions.
The above supplication relates to this incident.

As with Prophet Muhammad[PBUH], many other nabis also
fought for Truth. All of them had invoked this supplication to
obtain victory against unbelievers. In response to this prayer,
ALLAH had granted them with *reward in this world and a better
reward in the Hereafter* (Al-i-'Imran 3:148).

*And He it is Who accepts the apology
of His bondsmen, and pardons the faults...*

(As-Shuara 42:25)

For increasing faith

رَبَّنَآ اٰمَنَّا بِمَآ اَنزَلْتَ وَاتَّبَعْنَا الرَّسُولَ فَاكْتُبْنَا مَعَ الشَّهِدِينَ ۞

Rabbanâ âmannâ bimâ anzalta wa-ttaba'na-r rasûla
fa-ktubnâ ma'a-sh shâhidîn.
Our RABB! we believe in what You had revealed, and we follow the
rasul; so enroll us with the bearers of witness. (Al-i-'Imran 3:53)

During turbulent times of life, the people with weaker faith
start wandering around. Some of us indulge in activities not
endorsed by ALLAH. This supplication helps us to overcome such
challenging situations. Prophet 'Isa^{PBH}, suspecting some disbelief
among his followers, enquired about the status of their faith
(*Al-i-'Imran* 3:52). Some of 'Isa's^{PBH} disciples were *Hawariyyun*, a
group of righteous people, who always wore white garments as
a sign for purity. These *Hawariyyun* invoked ALLAH with this *du'a*
to include them as witness to the truth.

Similar to the *Hawariyyun*, we also know that successful are
those who bear the witness to truth. While we testify our faith,
we also show our commitment by action—following the path
shown by the Rasul^{PBUH}.

...We have not neglected anything in the Scripture...

(Al-An'am 6:38)

For honor on the Day of Awakening

رَبَّنَا وَاٰتِنَا مَا وَعَدتَّنَا عَلٰى رُسُلِكَ وَلَا تُخْزِنَا يَوْمَ الْقِيٰمَةِ ۗ اِنَّكَ لَا تُخْلِفُ الْمِيْعَادَ ۞

Rabbanâ wa âtinâ mâ wa'adtanâ 'alâ rusulika wa lâ tukhzinâ yawma-l qiyâmat. Innaka lâ tukhlifu-l mî'âd.

Our RABB! and give us what You have promised us through Your rasuls, and do not disgrace us on the day of Awakening. Surely You do not break promise. (Al-i-'Imran 3:194)

This prayer is part of a series of four supplications (pages 14, 15, and 35). These supplications are invoked by those people who remember ALLAH, whether they are sitting, standing or lying on their sides (*Al-i-'Imran* 3:191).

The rasuls brought promises of peace, justice and prosperity. Not only that, the rasuls brought the glad tidings for the believers. Those who follow the path guided by the rasuls will eventually emerge successful. As true Muslims, since we follow our Rasul[PBUH], we do not want to be disgraced on the Day of Awakening. While attaining the objectives of peace, justice and prosperity, let us not forget the other life—the life in the Hereafter. The verse that follows these four prayers confirms that ALLAH *immediately responds* to these supplications, and rewards the believers with entry to the *Gardens beneath which flow the rivers.* Do we need any further stimulus when ALLAH promises immediate response to these prayers?

...The promise of ALLAH. ALLAH does not fail in promise.

(Az-Zumar 39:20)

For honor on the Day of Awakening

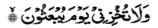

Wa lâ tu<u>kh</u>zinî yawma yub'a<u>th</u>ûn.
And do not disgrace me on the day when they are raised. (As-Shu'ara 26:87)

This supplication is part of a series of supplications (see page 87) made by Ibrahim[PBH].

On the Day of Judgment, people would be sorted into three groups: the righteous, the wrongdoers and the Foremost (*Al-Waqi'ah* 56:7-10). The Foremost and the righteous will be honored on this Day while the wrongdoers will be disgraced. Everybody will receive their full dues, and the guilty can not escape consequences of their deeds.

Although Ibrahim[PBH] is of the Foremost of the Muslims, out of humility he is seeking protection from being disgraced on the Day of Judgment. We should invoke ALLAH with this prayer to include us with the righteous people so that we are not disgraced into the hell. As we exert to become reverent and righteous, ALLAH rewards by bringing the Garden close to us (*As-Shu'ara* 26:90). In verse 26:104, in response to these supplications, ALLAH assures that He is *indeed the Exalted in might, most Rewarding.*

...if it were of the weight of a seed of mustard,
We shall bring it forth...

(Al-Anbiya' 21:47)

For believers

رَبَّنَا اغْفِرْ لِي وَلِوَالِدَيَّ وَلِلْمُؤْمِنِينَ يَوْمَ يَقُومُ الْحِسَابُ ۞

Rabbana-ghfir lî wa li-wâlidayya wa li-l mu'minîna
yawma yaqûmu-l hisâb.

*Our RABB! protect me and my parents and the Believers — on the
day when the reckoning is set up.* (Ibrahim 14:41)

This is part of a series of supplications (see pages 8 and
18) invoked by Ibrahim[PBH]. In this extraordinary supplication
Ibrahim[PBH] is not only asking protection for him and his parents,
but for all the believers against hellfire. This is truly an ideal
supplication to be invoked daily due to its generous inclusion
of all.

Ibrahim[PBH] was a kind hearted person (*At-Taubah* 9:114), and
we have much to learn from him. As he did, we should include
others in our prayers so that our RABB grants His mercy to all the
believers. The requested protection is not limited to the day of
Reckoning, but also for protection on this earth. Unless we avoid
sins in this life, how can we expect full protection on the Day of
Judgment?

*...whoever does good—out of a male or a female, and
is a Believer,—then these will enter the Garden,...*

(Al-Mu'min 40:40)

For believers

دَرِّ اغْفِرْ لِى وَلِوَالِدَىَّ وَلِمَنْ دَخَلَ بَيْتِىَ مُؤْمِنًا وَّلِلْمُؤْمِنِيْنَ
وَالْمُؤْمِنْتِ وَلَا تَزِدِ الظّلِمِيْنَ إِلَّا تَبَارًا ۝

Rabbi-ghfir lî wa li-wâlidayya wa liman dakhala
baytiya mu'minan wa li-l mu'minîna wa-l mu'minât. Wa
lâ tazidi-z zâlimîna illâ tabârâ.

*My RABB! forgive me and my parents, and whoever enters my house
as a Believer, and the believing men and the believing women. And do
not increase the wrongdoers in anything but destruction.* (Nuh 71:28)

ALLAH had rescued Nuh[PBH] and his few followers from the
massive deluge. When the water subsided, Nuh[PBH] asked for
forgiveness for the believers. He also asked for destruction of
the wrongdoers. This is not an expression of hatred or a sadistic
approach. Law and order cannot come to a land unless the
wicked are punished.

The torment, death, destruction during the deluge forced
everybody to evaluate their past misdeeds. Although Nuh[PBH] is
a prophet, and a sinless person (*Al-i-'Imran* 3:161), he requested
forgiveness for any faults. The surviving believers may not have
been sinless, and Nuh[PBH] worried about further punishment.
Therefore, he pleaded a respite, as he was not seeking another
ordeal of hanging on to an Ark.

When we repeat this supplication for forgiveness, we plead
for our parents and all the believers along with us. Our effort
to become *muttaqi* must be a teamwork. When we help others to
climb the mountain of faith, we simultaneously scale it before
we realize.

...My reward is with none but ALLAH...

(As-Saba' 34:37)

For disassociating from sinners

رَبِّ إِنِّى لَآ اَمْلِكُ إِلَّا نَفْسِى وَاَخِى فَافْرُقْ بَيْنَنَا وَبَيْنَ الْقَوْمِ الْفٰسِقِيْنَ ۞

Rabbi innî lâ amliku illâ nafsî wa akhî fa-fruq baynanâ
wa bayna-l qawmi-l fâsiqîn.

*My RABB! surely I have no control except on myself and my
brother, therefore make a separation between us and between the
disobedient people* (Al-Ma'idah 5:25).

Musa[PBH] was planning to enter the holy land of Canaan
along with the Israelites. He had developed a strategy based
on the information provided by spies. A large number of his
community panicked and resisted such an idea. They even
renounced their trust on ALLAH.

Musa[PBH] realized that he wields little control over these
disobedient people. He, as a prophet, could foresee a punishment
was surely looming. Therefore, he pleaded to ALLAH to separate
the true believers from the disobedient people. In response,
ALLAH restricted the land of Canaan from the insolent people
virtually for their lifetime.

By repeating this supplication, we seek ALLAH's help to draw
a barrier between the disobedient people and us. Thus, we are
trying to eliminate the wrong influence and evil company of
ungodly people.

...neither good nor evil can become parallel...

(Fussilat 41:34)

SUPPLICATION BY THE POTENTIAL PUNISHED

For disassociating from sinners

رَبَّنَا لَا تَجْعَلْنَا مَعَ الْقَوْمِ الظَّلِمِينَ ۞

Rabbanâ lâ taj'alnâ ma'a-l qawmi-z zâlimîn.
Our Rabb! do not place us along with the unjust community. (Al-
A'raf 7:47)

Every good deed harvests a reward and every bad deed
a punishment. Many people are not totally pious—they have
performed many good deeds, but have blemishes on their
records. These people would be watching their fate for the
permission to the heaven (*Al-A'raf* 7:46). They will worry if they
are destined to the Fire for their sins. They will plead ALLAH to
separate them from the unjust community and assign them to
the heaven: the ultimate reward for the pious.

The unjust communities around us continually betray the
faith and entertain evil actions. If we freely associate with them,
our chance to commit sins increases. We are not necessarily
perfect and therefore, we do not know if ultimately we will be
granted the Paradise. If ALLAH accepts this supplication from us,
He will distinguish us from the sinners and allow us entry into
the heaven.

And it is alike to them whether you warn them
or you do not warn them,—they will not believe.

(Ya-Sin 36:10)

For disassociating from sinner

عَلَى اللهِ تَوَكَّلْنَا رَبَّنَا لَا تَجْعَلْنَا فِتْنَةً لِّلْقَوْمِ الظَّالِمِينَ ۞ وَنَجِّنَا بِرَحْمَتِكَ مِنَ الْقَوْمِ الْكَافِرِينَ ۞

'Ala-llâhi tawakkalnâ; Rabbanâ lâ taj'alnâ fitnatan li-l qawmi-z zâlimîn. Wa najjinâ bi-rahmatika mina-l qawmi-l kâfirîn.

Upon ALLAH we do rely. Our RABB! do not make us a trial for the unjust people; And rescue us with Your mercy from the Unbelieving people. (Yunus 10:85-86)

Trials of life could be extreme for the unjust people. If we are roped into such trials, these may become unbearable for us.

As the community continually rejected Musa[PBH], few brave and righteous youths renounced Pharaoh. Although these youths apprehended severe persecution by the oppressive ruler, they correctly trusted that ALLAH's wish would prevail. Pharaoh threatened to punish them by crucifixion and cutting off legs on opposite directions. These youths did not falter; as they knew that ALLAH is the Best of all rescuers.

Historically, similar oppressive situations have been repeated, even today. When people in power victimize us, this prayer brings confidence in our heart towards ALLAH and His mercy.

This is an ideal prayer to invoke even before any trial befalls on us.

...the birds with wings outspread—each one knows its own Salat and its glorification...

(An-Nur 24:41)

For disassociating from sinners

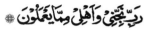

Rabbi najjinî wa ahlî mimmâ ya'malûn.
My RABB! deliver me and my followers from what they do. (As-Shu'ara' 26:169)

ALLAH blessed His creations with justice: good people are rewarded with bounties and the evil people are disciplined. However, the evil people are never caught unaware. They are informed and advised of the right path that would lead them to bliss. Even then, if they resist heeding, they receive further warnings. All these are meant for the benefit of the sinners. Justice cannot, however, permit continual practice of evil and rejection of warnings. The Qur'ân reminds us the fates of many such heedless communities.

Lut's^{PBH} community was corrupt, and they practiced the abhorrent act of approaching people of the same gender. As Lut^{PBH} repeatedly advised them against such practices, these people threatened him with expulsion from the two cities of Sodom and Gomorrah. Their repulsive acts and refusal to accept the guided path ceased their right to exist. Their absence would only help the righteous to practice guidance without distraction.

Lut^{PBH} had prayed this supplication to protect him and his true followers from ensuing destruction of the sinners. His prayer was successful, as the community perished in a fierce rain of fire from a volcanic eruption.

Around us today, we are observing abhorrent acts practiced and endorsed regularly. Is a catastrophe waiting to happen? May be. Let us pray for our safety before it is too late.

For disassociating from sinners

Rabbi najjinî mina-l qawmi-z zâlimîn.

My RABB! rescue me from the unjust people. (Al-Qasas 28:21)

When we try to establish peace and order, unjust people may become hell bent to disrupt peace. Musa^{PBH} had tried to resolve a fight but inadvertently killed an Egyptian (see page 30). Next day he found the surviving Israelite involved in yet another fight. Musa^{PBH} intervened again, but the discord did not resolve. Musa's^{PBH} intention was to establish peace, but the chiefs were trying to hunt him down. Anxious Musa^{PBH} escaped and invoked ALLAH to rescue him. ALLAH protected him and gave him shelter in Madyan (see page 54).

Repeatedly, we find that unjust people are getting an upper hand against us even though we are treading the right path. This supplication will help us overcome such situations.

To counter the unjust people, the *zâlims*, we must not become *zâlim*. ALLAH does not help the *zâlims*, He showers mercy on the righteous.

...do not despair the mercy of ALLAH.
Surely ALLAH forgives the sins altogether...

(Az-Zumar 39:53)

For disassociating from sinners

Rabbi-nṣurnî 'ala-l qawmi-l mufsidîn.

My RABB! help me against the mischievous people. (Al-'Ankabut 29:30)

Usually sin is not solitary, but flourish with and feed other evil actions. How can we expect success if we associate with the sinners?

The people of Lut's^PBH community were not only perverts, but also highway robbers and corrupt in governmental activities. Temporary gains from their sins made them arrogant. Even Lut's^PBH wife was against him. They all laughed at Lut's^PBH warnings and challenged a chastisement from ALLAH, if such an Authority existed!

As the community seemed unbearable and difficult to handle, Lut^PBH invoked his RABB to help him from the evil people. Just as other sincere supplications, this one was also accepted. A punishment in the form of volcanic eruption turned the town upside down and eliminated this pervert community.

Temptations may be hard to resist, but little help from ALLAH guides us to avoid such evil path.

...if you revere ALLAH He will give you a Discrimination, and wipe off from you your evils, and protect you...

(Al-Anfal 8:29)

For disassociating from sinners

رَّبِّ إِمَّا تُرِيَنِّي مَا يُوعَدُونَ ۞ رَبِّ فَلَا تَجْعَلْنِي فِي الْقَوْمِ
الظَّلِمِينَ ۞

Rabbi immâ turiyannî mâ yû'adûn. Rabbi fa-lâ taj'alnî
fi-l qawmi-z zâlimîn.

*My RABB! should You show me what they are promised,—my
RABB! Then do not place me with the unjust people.* (Al-Mu'minun
23:93-94)

ALLAH taught Muhammad[PBUH] to invoke Him with these
words. The promise of ALLAH is to serve justice: reward for
every good deed, and discipline for the bad. For perpetual evil,
they—the unjust people, are promised a show of destruction.
When the show begins its violent form, will it selectively pick
the participants? A Divine calamity is not an utter chaos,
rather an outcome with surgical precision. When the tumor of
the society was to be resected, Our Rasul[PBUH] pleaded a rescue
from the scalpel. In the following verse (*Al-Mu'minun* 23:95),
ALLAH affirms that He has every expertise to carry out a precise
punishment to the wrongdoers.

Surely wrongdoers will be punished, unless their repentance
earns mercy. We should pray to ALLAH to distinguish us when
forthcoming calamities will grip the unbelievers.

ALLAH's punishment is never a defective guided missile that
misses the target. This *du'a* will distance us from the target of
the punishment.

...surely the promise of ALLAH is true...

(Al-Fatir 35:5)

For disassociating from sinners

Rabbi lâ ta<u>dh</u>ar 'ala-l ar<u>d</u>i mina-l kâfirîna dayyârâ.

My RABB! do not leave on the land any inhabitant of the Unbelievers.
(Nuh 71:26)

Nuh^{PBH} was a prophet in Iraq to a community that was idol-worshipper. This community worshipped *Wadd, Suwa, Yaghuth, Ya'uq* and *Nasr*—a male deity, a female deity, a lion, a horse and an eagle respectively (*Nuh* 71:23). This community vehemently resisted Nuh's^{PBH} preaching of worshipping One and Only unseen God. After this community was destroyed, Nuh^{PBH} established a new community with some believers. As these people were on the right path, peace and justice were in the horizon.

Nuh^{PBH} prayed to ALLAH to eradicate all unbelievers from this newly established community. If any unbeliever accepts the truth, that is so much better. He reasoned that unbelievers will only mislead the believers into doing wrongful acts. For the best of his community, Nuh^{PBH} did not want to see any traces of unbelievers. The believers who were rescued from the deluge must get every opportunity to practice reverence. Nuh^{PBH} could not allow such opportunities be marred by unbelievers again.

*And beware of a calamity which does not smite
exclusively those among you who do wrong...*

(Al-Anfal 8:25)

For dying in righteousness

رَبَّنَآ أَفْرِغْ عَلَيْنَا صَبْرًا وَتَوَفَّنَا مُسْلِمِينَ ﴿

Rabbanâ afri<u>gh</u> 'alaynâ <u>s</u>abra<u>n</u> wa tawaffanâ muslimîn.

Our R<small>ABB</small>! pour upon us perseverance, and cause us to die as Muslims. (Al-A'raf 7:126)

Some of us may have been in such challenging situations that our faith is tested with our lives. In the face of death or near-death situations, we need monumental patience and assurance of A<small>LLAH</small>'s mercy.

The high officials of Pharaoh's court confronted a similar situation. These officials and magicians were in a heated debate with Musa^{PBH}. Musa's^{PBH} arguments were so convincing (see page 88) that these wise men became believers. Pharaoh was shocked to see this development amongst his own employees. He threatened to kill them by crucifixion and by other means of torturous death.

Although the supplication appears short, it reflects the anxiety of these new Muslims. They had worked for Pharaoh and knew very well that he would not spare them. They also knew that it would be humanly impossible to bear the physical torture unless A<small>LLAH</small> provides them abundant *sabr* or perseverance. They did not falter, they would rather die being Muslims than leading a sinful life with Pharaoh.

This *du'a* will help us endure difficult political conditions and fortify our faith even in the face of extreme opposition.

...And A<small>LLAH</small> loves the persevering.

(Al-i-'Imran 3:147)

For dying in righteousness

رَبِّ قَدْ اٰتَيْتَنِيْ مِنَ الْمُلْكِ وَعَلَّمْتَنِيْ مِنْ تَأْوِيْلِ الْأَحَادِيْثِ ۚ فَاطِرَ
السَّمٰوٰتِ وَالْأَرْضِ ۖ اَنْتَ وَلِيّ فِى الدُّنْيَا وَالْاٰخِرَةِ ۚ تَوَفَّنِيْ مُسْلِمًا وَّالْحِقْنِيْ
بِالصّٰلِحِيْنَ ۝

Rabbi qad âtaytanî mina-l mulki wa 'allamtanî min
ta'wîli-l aḥâdîthi; fâṭira-s samâwâti wa-l arḍi, anta waliyyî
fi-d dunyâ wa-l âkhirat; tawaffanî musliman wa al-ḥiqnî
bi-s ṣâliḥîn.

*My RABB! You have already given me of the kingdom and taught me
the interpretation of the narratives; Originator of the heavens and the
earth! You are my Protector in this world and the Hereafter. Make me
die as a Muslim, and join me with the righteous.* (Yusuf 12:101)

Yusuf^{PBH} had invoked this *du'a* after he became a top official
of Egypt, and was reunited with his parents. Yusuf^{PBH} was not
a king but a senior member of the kingdom, yet he compared
his position as if his RABB gave him a kingdom. Similarly, in our
daily life, we may not own a real kingdom, but many of us are
fortunate to own lots of riches, wealth and social position. Each
of us therefore can be compared to owning a kingdom.

After seeing the long-lost son, the parents prostrated to ALLAH
in gratitude, and Yusuf^{PBH} realized his dream of eleven stars and
the sun and the moon making prostration. Although Yusuf^{PBH}
received worldly affluence, he asked for last breath in the state of
a Muslim. Death in righteousness is a better achievement than
owning a kingdom.

How much would our prosperity mean if we do not die as
Muslims and most importantly, if we are not with the righteous
in the Hereafter?

He it is Who causes life and causes death...

(Al-Mu'min 40:68)

For dying in righteousness

رَبَّنَا عَلَيْكَ تَوَكَّلْنَا وَإِلَيْكَ اَنَبْنَا وَإِلَيْكَ الْمَصِيرُ ۞

Rabbanâ 'alayka tawakkalnâ wa ilayka anabnâ wa ilayka-l maṣîr.

Our RABB! upon You do we rely, and towards You do we turn, and towards You is the eventual coming. (Al-Mumtahanah 60:4)

Since the RABB is our Destination, rebellion against Him is impractical. Our works and thoughts in this life should thus be aimed towards a complete submission.

Ibrahim[PBH] and his followers—who were *good examples* (*Al-Mumtahanah* 60:4,6), invoked this supplication. Ibrahim's[PBH] sire Azar was a polytheist and refused to accept the Unity of ALLAH. Being a tenderhearted, forbearing person (*At-Taubah* 9:114), Ibrahim[PBH] had asked ALLAH to forgive Azar. Azar, however, persisted his rebellion, for which he was branded as an enemy of ALLAH. Ibrahim[PBH] and his followers knew that polytheism can never be the right way. They relied on ALLAH, and faced strong opposition by Azar and his group. ALLAH's authority is all inclusive of this world and the Hereafter, and this clear understanding is reflected in this supplication.

This prayer shows sincerity of our souls and it should be part of our daily supplications to ALLAH.

Those whom the angels will cause to die in pure state, saying: "Salam be upon you..."

(An-Nahl 16:32)

Acceptance of efforts

$$ \text{رَبَّنَا تَقَبَّلْ مِنَّا إِنَّكَ أَنْتَ السَّمِيعُ الْعَلِيمُ} \circledast $$

Rabbanâ taqabbal minnâ. Innaka anta-s samî'u-l 'alîm.

Our RABB! accept from us. You indeed, You are the all-Hearing, the all-Knowing. (Al-Baqarah 2:127)

Ibrahim[PBH] and son Isma'il[PBH] raised the foundation of the House of Ka'bah. During the construction, both of them invoked ALLAH to accept their efforts. ALLAH granted their desires and made the Ka'bah our *Qiblah* and spiritual center of entire Muslim world. Ibrahim[PBH] and Isma'il[PBH] did not live long enough to see the full extent of the reward of this prayer. Millions of people make pilgrimage to the Ka'bah every year and many more turn towards it everyday for their salat.

We should invoke this *du'a* whenever we initiate any project or effort. Like many other, this supplication has two parts. The first part is the pleading and the second part is a qualification of ALLAH. This verse confirms that ALLAH is all Hearing and all Knowing. ALLAH knows our desires that we have not verbally expressed, and He listens to every word that we speak. He is with us in our every effort and every walk. He is there to help, but how often do we ask? Our simple request can bring great reward to any good effort.

As a compiler of this book, I am reciting this verse to accept my small effort to inspire others with these beautiful supplications from the Qur'ân.

Whoever brings good, he will then have better than it...

(Al-Qasas 28:84)

Seeking shelter

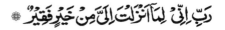

Rabbi innî limâ anzalta ilayya min khairin faqîr.

My RABB! I am indeed needy of whatever good You may send to me.
(Al-Qasas 28:24)

Musa^{PBH} had reached the desert of Madyan while escaping from Pharaoh. There he saw some men were watering animals from a well while two helpless women were waiting for the water. Although Musa^{PBH} was tired from the ordeal of escape, he helped these women fetch water and then sat down under the shade of a tree. The cool shade brought some relief, and he invoked the RABB referring to the shade as *whatever good*.

ALLAH's response followed quickly. One of the two women came back with an invitation from their old father. Their father was patriarch Shuaib^{PBH} (Jethro) who kindly offered a shelter and employment to Musa^{PBH}. Prophet Shuaib^{PBH} was impressed and eventually married Safura, one of the daughters, to Musa^{PBH}.

Let us explore little more on the far-reaching blessings from this supplication. Musa^{PBH} settled down and established his family in Madyan. Madyan is located near Mt. Sinai where Musa^{PBH} received his revelations. Although Musa^{PBH} apparently asked for a mere shade of a tree, ALLAH provided him long-term shelter, a family, an employment and ultimately the prophethood. Instead of specifying a shade of a tree, or a hut, or a house, Musa^{PBH} left the decision with his RABB to determine whatever would be good for a traveler.

Would it not be better for us to leave the decision-making on ALLAH by invoking this inspiring supplication instead of specifying for a particular job, a business contract, or a material object? ALLAH the most Merciful might give us much more than our myopic wishes.

Seeking forgiveness

رَبَّنَا ظَلَمْنَا أَنفُسَنَا وَإِن لَّمْ تَغْفِرْ لَنَا وَتَرْحَمْنَا لَنَكُونَنَّ مِنَ الْخَاسِرِينَ ۞

Rabbanâ zalamnâ anfusanâ, wa in lam taghfir lanâ wa tarhamnâ la-nakûnanna mina-l khâsirîn.

Our RABB! we have done wrong to ourselves; and if You do not forgive us and have mercy on us, we shall surely become of the losers. (Al-A'raf 7:23)

Most probably, this is the first supplication invoked by any human. Shaitan had lured Adam^{PBH} and his wife when they were in the garden. Both of them failed to resist and slipped into error. In verse 7:22, we find that ALLAH admonished them for their wrong-doings.

In repentance, both Adam^{PBH} and his wife pleaded to ALLAH with this supplication. Even though they were early human beings, they both knew that ALLAH is the only recourse, and with ALLAH remains the forgiveness. Most Merciful ALLAH gave them and their progeny a place of rest and spiritual guidance. For thousands of years, descendants of Adam^{PBH} have repeated this supplication to ALLAH Almighty to forgive their all wrongdoings and to be merciful on them.

...and let them (possessor of grace and abundance) forgive and forget...

(An-Nur 24:22)

Seeking forgiveness

رَبَّنَا لَا تُؤَاخِذْنَا إِن نَّسِينَا أَوْ أَخْطَأْنَا رَبَّنَا وَلَا تَحْمِلْ عَلَيْنَا إِصْرًا كَمَا حَمَلْتَهُ عَلَى الَّذِينَ مِن قَبْلِنَا رَبَّنَا وَلَا تُحَمِّلْنَا مَا لَا طَاقَةَ لَنَا بِهِ وَاعْفُ عَنَّا وَاغْفِرْ لَنَا وَارْحَمْنَا أَنتَ مَوْلَانَا فَانصُرْنَا عَلَى الْقَوْمِ الْكَافِرِينَ ۝

Rabbanâ lâ tuâ'khiznâ in nasînâ aw akhta'nâ; Rabbanâ wa lâ tahmil 'alaynâ isran kamâ hamaltahû 'ala-l ladhîna min qablinâ; Rabbanâ wa lâ tuhammilnâ mâ lâ tâqata lanâ bihi; wa-'fu 'annâ, wa-ghfir lanâ, wa-rhamnâ, anta mawlânâ fa-nsurnâ 'ala-l qawmi-l kâfirîn.

Our RABB! do not take us to task if we forget, or we make a mistake; our RABB! and do not lay upon us a burden as you had lain on those before us; our RABB! and do not impose upon us that for which no strength have we. Therefore, pardon us; and grant us protection; and be kind to us. You are our Patron; therefore help us over the Unbelieving people. (Al- Baqarah 2:286)

This is the concluding verse of Surah *Al-Baqarah*. The value of this *du'a* is realized as "whoever prays as taught in the last two verses of the *Baqarah* at night, they are sufficient for him" (*Sahih Bukhari* 5.59.345, 6.61.530,571). Although this supplication seeks forgiveness, it also stresses the need to be humble and the need to protect us from evil.

Our limitations are explicit to ALLAH. He is not a harsh master, rather a kind Guide. Holding our hands, He crosses us through darkness. He guides us to practice sincerity and humility: two virtues that are emphasized in this prayer. Once humble, we will not be handicapped with unbearable burden. When we qualify to receive ALLAH's forgiveness, we will gain help over the Unbelieving people.

Fair speech and pardoning are better than charity followed by injury...

(Al-Baqarah 2:263)

Seeking forgiveness

رَبَّنَآ اِنَّنَآ اٰمَنَّا فَاغْفِرْلَنَا ذُنُوْبَنَا وَقِنَا عَذَابَ النَّارِ ۚ

Rabbanâ innanâ âmannâ fa-ghfir lanâ dhunûbanâ wa qinâ 'adhâba-n nâr.

Our RABB! we have certainly believed; therefore forgive us of our sins, and save us from the punishment of the Fire. (Al-i-'Imran 3:16)

Sincere belief will be amply rewarded on the Day of Judgment: the believer will arrive with a clean slate, devoid of any blemishes. In this supplication the desired reward for the true believer is firstly forgiveness of sins, and then the safety from the hellfire.

This supplication is invoked by Muslims who are patient, true in their action, devout and are charitable. Each of these characteristics is praised and encouraged in Islam. Invoking a supplication by itself is never adequate. We have to practice what we preach. Like a humble acorn, we must hold the ground and weather the seasons to flourish into the greatest oak. When our words are reflected in our actions, and we practice patience like the acorn, we will find that ALLAH is oft-Returning, most Kind. He will help us to flourish with greatest *imaan*.

...Do you not love that ALLAH should forgive you?...

(An-Nur 24:22)

Seeking forgiveness

رَبِّ إِنِّىٓ أَعُوذُ بِكَ أَنْ أَسْئَلَكَ مَالَيْسَ لِى بِهِ عِلْمٌ وَإِلَّا تَغْفِرْ لِى وَتَرْحَمْنِىٓ أَكُن مِّنَ الْخَٰسِرِينَ ۝

Rabbi innî a'ûdhu bika an as-a'laka mâ laysa lî bihî 'ilm. Wa illâ taghfir-lî wa tarhamnî akun mina-l khâsirîn.

My RABB! surely I seek refuge with You for asking You that about which I have no knowledge; and if You do not forgive me and have mercy to me, I shall become of the losers. (Hud 11:47)

In our distress, we make supplications that may be either inappropriate or made on behalf of evil people.

At the time of Great Deluge, Nuh^{PBH} had requested ALLAH to save his son on the pretext that the son was a member of the family. Nuh's^{PBH} request was out of fatherly love for his son (*Hud* 11:45). However, this son was a sinner and rejecter of faith, and was not to be saved. ALLAH admonished Nuh^{PBH} for asking about which he has no knowledge (*Hud* 11:46).

This supplication expresses humility in our mind and seeks forgiveness and guidance from ALLAH. We admit that we know so little about the unknown and unseen. To ALLAH we seek refuge and guidance—without which we shall become of the losers. This prayer is a complete submission to Almighty ALLAH for His mercy and guidance.

This incident reminds that supplications made on behalf of evil people are not accepted. Further, ALLAH does not accept prayers made with bad intentions and He does not support evil designs.

...Sufficient is ALLAH as an Accountant.

(Al-Ahzab 33:39)

Seeking forgiveness

لَّا إِلَهَ إِلَّا أَنتَ سُبْحَنَكَ إِنِّى كُنتُ مِنَ الظَّلِمِينَ ۞

Lâ ilâha illâ anta sub<u>h</u>ânaka; innî kuntu mina-<u>z</u> <u>z</u>âlimîn.

There is no deity but You, glory be to You! Surely I became among the unjust. (Al-Anbiya 21:87)

Yunus^{PBH} preached to the people of Nineveh, a town in Mawsil situated in Northern Iraq. While preaching the message of God, he became distraught as his people refused to accept the Truth. As a prophet, he should not have resigned but remained persistent in spite of the initial failures. Out of frustration, Yunus^{PBH} abandoned his people and boarded a ship. During the voyage, the sailors assumed Yunus^{PBH} had brought bad omen and threw him off the ship. Distressed Yunus^{PBH} sincerely begged forgiveness stating that *surely* he was *unjust* in abandoning his community.

The following verse mentions that ALLAH responded and delivered Yunus^{PBH} from the grief. It also tells us that ALLAH will deliver the believers in a similar fashion (if they make sincere repentance and seek forgiveness). In our everyday life, we make mistakes and commit sins. If we sincerely repent and amend ourselves, then surely ALLAH is most Merciful and Forgiving.

...those who fear their RABB in secret, there is for them forgiveness and a great reward.

(Al-Mulk 67:12)

Seeking forgiveness

رَبَّنَا اغْفِرْ لَنَا وَلِإِخْوَانِنَا الَّذِينَ سَبَقُونَا بِالْإِيمَانِ وَلَا تَجْعَلْ فِي قُلُوبِنَا غِلًّا لِلَّذِينَ آمَنُوا رَبَّنَا إِنَّكَ رَءُوفٌ رَّحِيمٌ ۞

Rabbana-ghfir lanâ wa li-ikhwânina-l ladhîna sabaqûnâ bil-îmâni wa lâ taj'al fî qulûbinâ ghillan li-l ladhîna âmanû rabbanâ innaka raū'fu-r rahîm.

Our RABB! forgive us, and our brethren who have preceded us in faith, and do not keep any spite in our hearts towards those who believe; our RABB! surely You are very Compassionate, most Rewarding. (Al-Hashr 59:10)

The Muslim *ummah* would prosper if we all take care of each other and do not keep any disliking against our brethrens.

During the time of the Prophet[PBUH], people were coming to the fold of Islam in batches. Some of the newer reverts had, in the past, expressed animosity towards Muslims. Now that all are Muslims, the new reverts invoked ALLAH for forgiveness of their past misdeeds. They desired forgiveness for their late acceptance of Islam. They knew that if they continue to possess previous ill-feelings, their sins would not be erased. Consequently, they pleaded the RABB to cleanse their heart of all kind of malice towards their brothers in faith.

...those who do an evil act in ignorance, then quickly turn; so these–ALLAH turns to them...

(An-Nisa' 4:17)

Seeking forgiveness

رَبَّنَآ أَتْمِمْ لَنَا نُورَنَا وَاغْفِرْ لَنَا ۖ إِنَّكَ عَلَىٰ كُلِّ شَيْءٍ قَدِيرٌ ۝

Rabbanâ atmim lanâ nûranâ wa-ghfir lanâ; innaka
'alâ kulli shayi'n qadîr.

*Our RABB! complete for us our Light, and forgive us; verily You are
Possessor of power over all things.* (At-Tahrim 66:8)

When the world is in spiritual darkness, Divine Light can
guide us towards the right path. The light of the Truth is bright
enough to pierce through any darkness. Yet, sins and arrogance
can create layers of cataract, forcing us to ignore the Truth as an
ostrich.

As a prelude to this supplication, ALLAH tells us that for the
righteous, the Light will always be in their front, guiding them
through the darkness so that they will not stumble upon any
sins. In this verse, ALLAH summons the believers for a sincere
turning, so that He may wipe off their sins.

When the Light is complete for us, and we are rightly guided,
may ALLAH forgive our all kinds of faults. Let ALLAH make us die
in the state of righteousness, so that we become immortal in the
Hereafter (*Ad-Dukhan* 44:56).

*Surely, ALLAH will not pardon that partners be
set up with Him, but besides that
He pardons whom He pleases...*

(An-Nisa' 4:48,116)

Protection from trial

رَبَّنَا لَا تَجْعَلْنَا فِتْنَةً لِّلَّذِينَ كَفَرُوا وَاغْفِرْ لَنَا رَبَّنَا إِنَّكَ أَنتَ الْعَزِيزُ الْحَكِيمُ ۞

Rabbanâ lâ taj'alnâ fitnatan li-ladhîna kafarū waghfir lanâ rabbanâ; innaka anta-l 'azîzu-l ḥakîm.

Our RABB! do not make us a trial for those who disbelieve, and forgive us, our RABB! truly You, only You are Exalted in Might, most Wise. (Al-Mumtahanah 60:5)

Ibrahim's[PBH] ancestor Azar was an idol-worshipper. In spite of repeated advice, Azar and his people refused to accept the Truth. Being kind-herated, Ibrahim[PBH] had prayed to ALLAH to forgive Azar. ALLAH, however, did not forgive Azar who was not willing to rectify an amend.

Ibrahim[PBH] knew that he would not prevail upon ALLAH to influence justice, and that a trial would be coming on the wrongdoers. Thus, he optimistically aspired for the Muslims a protection against the trial. He also appealed for forgiveness for any mistakes, including the request to save Azar.

This incident, as the one mentioned about Nuh[PBH] in page 58, reminds us that not all supplications are accepted, particularly if we plead on behalf of evildoers who are not willing to be guided.

Certainly ALLAH does not do injustice
to mankind in anyway...

(Yunus 10:44)

Against natural calamities

رَبِّ لَوْشِئْتَ اَهْلَكْتَهُمْ مِّنْ قَبْلُ وَاِيَّايَ ۚ اَتُهْلِكُنَا بِمَافَعَلَ السُّفَهَآءُ مِنَّا ۚ اِنْ هِيَ
اِلَّا فِتْنَتُكَ ۚ تُضِلُّ بِهَا مَنْ تَشَآءُ وَتَهْدِىْ مَنْ تَشَآءُ ۚ اَنْتَ وَلِيُّنَا فَاغْفِرْلَنَا
وَارْحَمْنَا وَاَنْتَ خَيْرُ الْغٰفِرِيْنَ ۞

Rabbi law <u>sh</u>i'ta ahlaktahum min qablu wa iyyâya.
A-tuhlikunâ bimâ fa'ala-s sufahâu' minnâ; in hiya
illâ fitnatuk. Tu<u>d</u>illu bihâ man ta<u>sh</u>âu' wa tahdî man
ta<u>sh</u>âu'. Anta waliyyunâ fa-<u>gh</u>fir lanâ wa-r<u>h</u>amnâ wa anta
<u>kh</u>ayru-l <u>gh</u>âfirîn.

*My RABB! if You had so wished, You could have destroyed them
before this, and me. Will You destroy us on account of what the foolish
among us have done? This is nothing but Your trial. You leave in
straying thereby whom You please and You guide whom You please.
You are our Protector, therefore forgive us and have Mercy on us, for
You are the Best of forgivers.* (Al-A'raf 7:155)

When Musa^{PBH} returned after his 40-days seclusion in the
mountain, he was angry and sad at the blasphemy of calf-
worshipping. As only ALLAH may punish such apostates, Musa^{PBH}
selected 70 men of unsound faith for ALLAH's tryst. While these
people were seized by an earthquake, Musa^{PBH} invoked this *du'a*
to rescue the innocent people.

When a large section of a community became engrossed in
sin, ALLAH wiped out the entire community through a natural
disaster or an epidemic. As the last Nabi^{PBUH} has passed away,
and mankind does not receive further warnings through
prophets, we do not for sure know if a contemporary natural
calamity is a punishment. Even then, we do not want to share
the punishments aimed towards the sinners.

...what will make you know what the Great Calamity is!

(Al-Qari'ah 101:3)

Expressing gratitude

رَبِّ أَوْزِعْنِيٓ أَنْ أَشْكُرَ نِعْمَتَكَ الَّتِيٓ أَنْعَمْتَ عَلَيَّ وَعَلَىٰ وَالِدَيَّ وَأَنْ أَعْمَلَ صَالِحًا تَرْضَـٰهُ وَأَصْلِحْ لِي فِي ذُرِّيَّتِيٓ إِنِّي تُبْتُ إِلَيْكَ وَإِنِّي مِنَ الْمُسْلِمِينَ ۞

Rabbi awzi'nî an ashkura ni'mataka-l latî an'amta 'alayya wa 'alâ wâlidayya wa an a'mala sâlihan tardâhu wa aslih lî fî dhurriyyati. Innî tubtu ilayka wa innî mina-l muslimîn.

My RABB! rouse me that I may give thanks for your favors with which you have favored upon me and upon my parents, and that I may do good — which may please you, and do good to me with regard to my offspring. Surely I turn to you, and I am indeed among the Muslims.
(Al-Ahqaf 46:15)

This and the next supplication are similar in content. At the core of both the prayers are gratitude and humbleness.

ALLAH relates in several preceding verses about the characteristics of believers and how they give thanks to ALLAH for His kindness. The verse that contains this supplication starts with a brief discussion on the process of birth. It particularly relates the pain that the mother tolerates during pregnancy and childbirth. As the verse indicates, parents' role does not end with childbirth, but a long nurturing period continues.

ALLAH tells this supplication is made by physically and spiritually mature people of age forty. As our awareness develops with age, we may be able to reach the humility to express our sincere thanks to all the favors that we received.

And if you count the favors of ALLAH, you will not be able to number them...

(An-Nahl 16:18)

Expressing gratitude

رَبِّ أَوْزِعْنِىٓ أَنْ أَشْكُرَ نِعْمَتَكَ الَّتِىٓ أَنْعَمْتَ عَلَىَّ وَعَلَىٰ وَالِدَىَّ وَأَنْ أَعْمَلَ
صَالِحًا تَرْضٰهُ وَأَدْخِلْنِى بِرَحْمَتِكَ فِى عِبَادِكَ الصّٰلِحِينَ ۞

Rabbi awzi'nî an ashkura ni'mataka-l latî an'amta
'alayya wa 'alâ wâlidayya wa an a'mala sâliha<u>n</u> tardâhu
wa ad<u>kh</u>ilnî bi-ra<u>h</u>matika fî 'ibâdika-<u>s</u> <u>s</u>âli<u>h</u>în.

*My RABB! permit me to give thanks for Your blessing which You
have bestowed on me and on my parents, and that I may do good which
pleases You, and admit me, with Your mercy, among Your righteous
bondsmen.* (An-Naml 27:19)

Sulaiman^{PBH} had invoked this supplication when he heard
worries from a member of the *Naml*. Compared to the weak and
insignificant *Naml*, Sulaiman^{PBH} was very powerful and majestic.
The fear of the *Namlites* made Sulaiman^{PBH} acknowledge the
blessings of ALLAH upon him. He would have been nothing had
not his parents brought him up with due care and education.
Therefore, he offers thanks to ALLAH for blessings on him as well
as on his parents.

The Qur'ân repeatedly commands people to do good to
others as well to oneself: a virtue that needs to be practiced.
This supplication specifically seeks ALLAH's mercy so that a
person can continue working towards good that pleases ALLAH.
Expression of gratitude is finest when worded with humility.
Sulaiman^{PBH}, although a powerful king, set a fine example of
humbleness in this supplication. In return of ALLAH's blessings,
he asked permission even to offer thanks. In addition, he offered
good deeds as a testimony of his gratitude.

...For those who do good there is good in this world...

(An-Nahl 16:30)

65

For safety in journey

بِسْمِ اللهِ مَجْرَبهَا وَمُرْسَبهَا ۚ إِنَّ رَبِّى لَغَفُورُرَّحِيمٌ ۞

Bismi-llâhi majrēhâ wa mursâhâ. Inna rabbî la-ghafûru-r rahîm.

With the name of ALLAH be its sailing and its anchoring. Surely my RABB is indeed Protector, most Rewarding. (Hud 11:41)

Nuh[PBH] prayed this supplication while he was sailing in his frail Ark. Towering waves of the great deluge were rocking the Ark violently. Many people on the ground, including Nuh's[PBH] own son, were washed away. This *du'a* reflects Nuh's[PBH] strong faith on the Protector during this tumultuous journey. The most Rewarding RABB listened to Nuh[PBH] and rewarded him with a safe and secure passage. We realize the achievement of this *du'a*, as Nuh[PBH] was not a professional ship-builder; he had crudely built the Ark with planks and nails (*Al-Qamar* 54:13). As a result of the prayer, the frail Ark sailed safely through the violent deluge. The Ark definitely needed the protection, which it obtained through this *du'a*, when it was in rough waters or even when it appeared safely anchored.

Although this supplication relates to the Ark, we can still pray to ALLAH to protect us in our cars or buses while in motion or while parked. ALLAH protects us during a flight or while the aircraft is stationery on the ground. As this prayer emphasizes, ALLAH is *surely* the Protector and most Rewarding.

How often we have trusted a bus driver or a pilot with our lives? Life is most secure when the Protector guards it from any kind of mishap from occurring. Our everyday commute is a sheer miracle from ALLAH considering accidents that lurk at every corner.

For safety in journey

رَبِّ أَدْخِلْنِى مُدْخَلَ صِدْقٍ وَّ أَخْرِجْنِى مُخْرَجَ صِدْقٍ وَاجْعَلْ لِّى مِنْ لَّدُنْكَ سُلْطَنًا نَّصِيرًا ۞

Rabbi a<u>kh</u>ilnî mud<u>kh</u>ala sidqi<u>n</u> wa a<u>kh</u>rijnî mu<u>kh</u>raja sidqi<u>n</u> wa-j'al lî mi<u>n</u> ladunka sul<u>t</u>ana<u>n</u> na<u>s</u>îrâ.

My RABB! make me enter a truthful entering, and bring me out a truthful bringing out, and grant me from Yourself an authoritative help.
(Bani Isra'il 17:80)

Prophet[PBUH] was in distress in Makkah and was planning to emigrate to safer Yathrib. At this time, ALLAH instructed the Nabi[PBUH] to invoke Him with this prayer.

The term *entering* indicates entry to Madinah, and *bringing out* is the departure from Makkah. The departure from Makkah and the incidents on the way, such as the spider's web at the cave entrance, were miraculous in nature. ALLAH rescues His slaves by careful planning without discounting Natural laws—yet such rescues are miraculous. Compared to the hostile attitude of the Makkans, the Madinites welcomed Prophet's[PBUH] entry to their township. The pleading for *authoritative help* resulted into future political success.

This supplication is highly appropriate for any endeavors, particularly during immigration to a new place or country. Immigration has always played an important role in Muslim world, demonstrated by the calendar system that starts with Prophet's[PBUH] immigration to Madinah.

If He wished He could still the wind, then they (ships) would become motionless...

(As-Shura 42:33)

For safety in journey

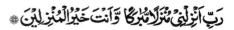

Rabbi anzilnî munzala**n** mubârakan wa anta <u>kh</u>ayru-l munzilîn.

My RABB! Make me land a blessed landing; for You are the Best of the disembarkers. (Al-Mu'minun 23:29)

ALLAH instructed Nuh[PBH] to invoke this prayer when getting down from the Ark after the deluge. As the hostile community was destroyed, Nuh[PBH] settled down with his true followers and a stock of farm animals to start a new community. Although safety in a journey is important, far more crucial are proper landing and our planned actions after that. A journey is usually short, but the life after the journey is most likely longer. If we reach a place safely, but the place is hostile to us or to Islam, then how good was the safety in journey?

This supplication is ideal before and during a journey, particularly if something is to be achieved at the completion of the trip.

...Travel in the earth, then see
how He originated the creation...

(Al-'Ankabut 29:20)

Against false accusation

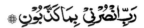

Rabbi-nsurnî bimâ kadhdhabûn.

My RABB! help me because they belie me. (Al-Mu'minun 23:26)

As unbelievers put up fierce opposition, only a stronger authority can counteract such hostility. At different occasions, all prophets had faced severe opposition. Surah *Al-Mu'minun,* which was revealed at Makkah, inspired our dear Prophet[PBUH] when he was under a humiliating situation. The surah narrates how Nuh[PBH] was comforted by ALLAH, and it continues to inspire us today when we are opposed and falsely accused.

As the community accused Nuh[PBH] of madness and falsehood, he turned to ALLAH for help. On the same topic, the Qur'ân also mentions similar yet different supplications (*Al-Qamar* 54:10, page 32; *As-Shu'ara'* 26:117, page 70). Thus, Nuh[PBH] had made several earnest pleadings. While the opposition of the unbelievers was severe, prayers of Nuh[PBH] were earnest, ALLAH's punishment on the unbelievers was stern and the reward to Nuh[PBH] was extraordinary.

It is a perfect supplication if a person initiates a good work and fears that people might react or reject the work. Others may stop us temporarily, but ALLAH helps us to progress eventually.

Woe be to every slanderer, defamer,

(Al-Humazah 104:1)

Against false accusation

رَبِّ إِنَّ قَوْمِى كَذَّبُونِ ۞ فَافْتَحْ بَيْنِى وَبَيْنَهُمْ فَتْحًا وَنَجِّنِى وَمَن مَّعِىَ مِنَ الْمُؤْمِنِينَ ۞

Rabbi inna qawmî ka<u>dhdh</u>abûn. Fa-ftah baynî wa baynahum fa<u>th</u>an wa najjinî wa man ma'iya mina-l mu'minîn.

My RABB! surely my people have belied me. Therefore You decide between me and between them a decision, and rescue me and those with me of the Believers. (As-Shu'ara' 26:117-118)

While all communities had resisted and ridiculed their prophets, Nuh's^{PBH} community was particularly ruthless. As a prologue to this supplication, ALLAH narrates the vicious attacks by the community towards Nuh^{PBH} and his few followers.

To the privileged class the mission of the prophets always seemed irrational, as most of the early followers were poor, oppressed and belonged to the lower class in the social system. The prosperous and privileged people even threatened Nuh^{PBH} of death by stoning (*As-Shu'ara'* 26:105-116).

Nuh's^{PBH} prayer to decide between him and the unbelievers was soon to be accepted. The punishment on the community and the rescue of the believers is well known and remains a Sign to the mankind (*As-Shu'ara'* 26:121). Even if people walking similar evil path fail to read the road signs, we know these signs assure justice.

This is an ideal prayer when a good work of a person is facing opposition from other people. The outcome of the good work must be good—hence, the supplication seeks goodly interference from ALLAH.

...and whoever does evil, it is then against it...

(Fussilat 41:46)

For provisions

رَبِّ اغْفِرْلِى وَهَبْ لِى مُلْكًا لَّا يَنْبَغِى لِاَحَدٍ مِّنْ بَعْدِى ۚ اِنَّكَ اَنْتَ الْوَهَّابُ ۞

Rabbi-ghfir lî wa hab lî mulkan lâ yanbaghî li-ahadin min ba'dî; innaka anta-l wahhâb.

My RABB! grant me protection, and grant me a kingdom which is not fit for anyone after me. Certainly You, You are the Great Giver.
(Sad 38:35)

Sulaiman's^{PBH} kingdom was secure except a temporary takeover by an infidel Jeroboam. When Sulaiman^{PBH} was successful in removing Jeroboam from the throne, he made this supplication to his RABB. He asked for protection, not only against future misadventure by rebels, but also against pitfalls as repentance is good but innocence is better. Sulaiman's^{PBH} kingdom was large and his wealth was legendary. He was anxious that after him, a crooked person as Jeroboam may take over and wreak havoc by using the large resources. In response to this supplication, the *Great Giver* increased material and spiritual wealth to Sulaiman^{PBH}. His fleets of ships sailed safely and quickly in favorable weather. Expert craftsmen such as divers and builders worked for him creating a vast fortune. After Sulaiman's^{PBH} death, nobody in Israel could inherit such a resourceful kingdom.

...We do not ask of you a provision,
We give sustenance to you...

(Ta Ha 20:132)

For provisions

اللهُمَّ رَبَّنَا آنْزِلْ عَلَيْنَا مَآئِدَةً مِّنَ السَّمَآءِ تَكُوْنُ لَنَا عِيْدًا لِّاَوَّلِنَا وَاٰخِرِنَا وَاٰيَةً
مِّنْكَ وَارْزُقْنَا وَاَنْتَ خَيْرُ الرَّزِقِيْنَ ۞

Allâhumma rabbanâ anzil 'alaynâ mâi'datan mina-s
samâi' taku'nu lanâ 'îdan li-awwalinâ wa âkhirinâ wa
âyatan minka; wa-rzuqnâ wa anta khayru-r râziqîn.

*O ALLAH! our RABB! send down upon us a Table Spread with Food
from heaven, that it may be to us an Eid for the first of us and for the
last of us, and a Sign from You; and provide sustenance to us, for You
are the Best of the sustainers* (Al-Ma'idah 5:114)

The Jewish community had challenged 'Isa^{PBH} to bring a
Table Spread of Food (*Al-Ma'idah* 5:112) from heaven, and if
this happened then they would believe 'Isa^{PBH} to be a genuine
prophet. On this, 'Isa^{PBH} pleaded his RABB to provide food for
soul and body. Such a humble supplication was accepted. The
following verse states that ALLAH sent ample food, and whoever
still refused to believe would receive a severe chastisement.
When ALLAH permits, there is abundant food, fit for an *Eid* (lit.
festival), for all of us. ALLAH is the Provider of our all sustenance,
be it for physical or for spiritual needs.

While we perform our jobs or business to bring bread on
our tables, it remains with ALLAH whether we are successful in
obtaining our livelihood. This is an ideal supplication to seek
blessings and sustenance from ALLAH, who has the ability to
provide endless supplies of provisions for our fulfillments.

*...And the provisions of your RABB
is better and more lasting.*

(Ta Ha 20:131)

For provisions

رَبَّنَا لَا تُزِغْ قُلُوبَنَا بَعْدَ إِذْ هَدَيْتَنَا وَهَبْ لَنَا مِن لَّدُنكَ رَحْمَةً إِنَّكَ أَنتَ الْوَهَّابُ ۞

Rabbanâ lâ tuzi<u>gh</u> qulûbanâ ba'da i<u>dh</u> hadaytanâ wa hab lanâ min ladunka ra<u>h</u>mata<u>n</u>; innaka anta-l wahhâb.

Our RABB! do not cause our hearts to deviate after You have guided us; and grant us mercy from Your Presence. Truly You, only You are the most liberal Giver. (Al-i-'Imran 3:8)

This supplication follows the verse that describes the two different types of verses in the Holy Qur'ân, i.e. Decisive and Allegorical. The people whose hearts are full of perversity seek trouble from the allegorical verses. While the steadfast in knowledge believe the whole Qur'ân.

The guidance in the Qur'ân is not limited to spiritual enhancement, but also for social justice, economic prosperity and political advancement. If we do not deviate from Islamic principles as outlined in the Qur'ân—equality of all human, identical justice for all, freedom in trade and business, quest for knowledge—then we will surely prosper and find ALLAH to be the *most liberal Giver* to all.

In this supplication, we are asking ALLAH, *the most liberal Giver,* to give us beyond our expectations. Once we receive guidance from ALLAH, it is our responsibility to continually follow that. The path to mercy is based on our constant effort to improve ourselves. Therefore, we are praying to ALLAH to protect us from slipping into sinful life after receiving the Guidance.

... both His hands are wide open,
He disburses as He pleases...

(Al-Ma'idah 5:64)

For granting Paradise

رَبَّنَا وَأَدْخِلْهُمْ جَنَّتِ عَدْنٍ الَّتِى وَعَدتَّهُمْ وَمَن صَلَحَ مِنْ ءَابَآئِهِمْ
وَأَزْوَاجِهِمْ وَذُرِّيَّتِهِمْ إِنَّكَ أَنتَ الْعَزِيزُ الْحَكِيمُ ۝

Rabbanâ wa adkhilhum jannâti 'adni ni-llatî
wa'adtahum wa man salaha min âbâi'him wa azwâjihim
wa dhurriyyâtihim. Innaka anta-l 'azîzu-l hakîm.

*Our RABB! and make them enter the Gardens of Eden, which You
have promised them, and those who do good from among their parents
and their spouses and their offspring. Certainly You Yourselves are
Exalted in Might, most Wise.* (Al-Mu'min 40:8)

The true Muslims and the angels, as the bearers of the
Throne of Power, plead to ALLAH to forgive all the believers. This
particular supplication is a part of three, the others are in pages
17 and 22. Some scholars understood the bearer of the *Throne of
Power* to signify angels only, while others feel that this term is
not exclusive to angels, but includes righteous humans who take
the responsibility to carry out all the commands arising from
the *Throne.*

The first supplication in this series pleads for forgiveness,
the present one is for granting paradise and the third one is
for protection against Shaitan. These supplications are truly
inspiring as they include all the fellow-beings of the bondsman:
parents, spouses and offspring.

*ALLAH has indeed purchased from the believers
their lives and their property, so that theirs is the
Garden...Therefore you rejoice on your bargain...*

(At-Taubah 9:111)

For perseverance

رَبَّنَآ أَفْرِغْ عَلَيْنَا صَبْرًا وَثَبِّتْ أَقْدَامَنَا وَانصُرْنَا عَلَى الْقَوْمِ الْكَفِرِينَ ۞

Rabbanâ afri<u>gh</u> 'alaynâ <u>s</u>abra<u>n</u> wa <u>th</u>abbit aqdâmanâ
wa-n<u>s</u>urnâ 'ala-l qawmi-l kâfirîn.

Our RABB! pour down upon us perseverance, and make our feet
firm, and help us against the unbelieving people. (Al-Baqarah 2:250)

All of us, some time in our lives, do face extraordinary odds
against us that crumble our patience and push our confidence
to a low ebb.

Such was the condition when Talut marched with his
soldiers to confront Jalut (Goliath). Before the battle, the small
force of Talut including Dawud^{PBH} made this supplication. Jalut
had more military resources: it was larger and stronger. In the
face of this enormous military imbalance, Talut had one key
advantage. ALLAH had responded to his supplication with divine
support. Talut's forces fought the battle with the authority of
ALLAH, Dawud^{PBH} killed Jalut, and ended his tyranny. For his
extraordinary patience, ALLAH rewarded Dawud^{PBH} with a
kingdom and wisdom (*Al-Baqarah* 2:251).

This supplication pleads for abundant *sabr* (lit. perseverance)
to face the odds. The path towards success is laid with bricks of
sabr. When darkness overtakes, patience can make us succesful
(*Al-'Asr* 103:3). With the guidance from ALLAH, if we can practice
perseverance, then we can turn the stumbling blocks into
stepping stones.

...persevere and excel in perseverance, and be persistent...

(Al-i-'Imran 3:200)

For parents

Rabbi-rhamhumâ kamâ rabbayânî saghîrâ.

My RABB! have mercy on them as they brought me up in the childhood. (Bani Isra'il 17:24)

All the supplications compiled in this book are from the Holy Qur'ân. Some of these are mentioned as prayed by prophets, others are prayed by pious Muslims and there are some, which are instructed by ALLAH Himself. This supplication, as taught by ALLAH, is a glorious example of human kindness.

The previous verse (*Bani Isra'il* 17:23) instructs us how to treat our elderly parents. These two verses exemplified generosity, and restrained even the mildest form of scorn.

As a prelude to this supplication, ALLAH instructs us to *lower our wings of humility out of tenderness* on our parents the way a mother bird protects her babies. We are indebted to our mother not only for the severe pangs of childbirth that she endured, but also to the unselfish acts of picking us up and cleaning us when we could not even turn ourselves. We depended on the parents for our upbringing until we started earning our livelihood, and arguably even beyond that.

When parents are elderly, it is for us to partially repay the debts—if we can do that. Even if we fail to offer physical help to our parents, should we not include this supplication in our daily prayers? If our parents have already passed away, this *du'a* seeks mercy for their souls.

...Give thanks to Me and to your parents...

(Luqman 31:14)

For offspring

رَبِّ هَبۡ لِى مِن لَّدُنكَ ذُرِّيَّةً طَيِّبَةً إِنَّكَ سَمِيعُ الدُّعَآءِ ۞

Rabbi hab-li` min ladunka dhurriyatan tayyibatan;
innaka samī'u-d du'âi'.

*My RABB! give me from Yourself a pure offspring. You are indeed
Hearer of prayer.* (Al-i-'Imran 3:38)

Mar-yam^{PBH} grew up under the care of her uncle,
Zakariyya^{PBH}. As she matured, she turned out to be an example
of purity and devoutness. As Zakariyya^{PBH} witnessed her
progress, he desired a child for himself—as pure, virtuous and
honorable as Mar-yam^{PBH}. Zakariyya^{PBH} was old and his wife
was barren, a combination that seemed unfit for parenthood.
Although ALLAH never breaks His own laws (*Al-Ahzab* 33:
62),—the laws of Nature—the variation of normal is within
the scope of these well-established laws. In the following verse
(*Al-i-'Imran* 3:39), angels brought the glad tidings of Yahya^{PBH}, *a
noble and a chaste man, and a nabi from among the righteous.* ALLAH
cured Zakariyya's^{PBH} wife from her barrenness and she was able
to bear a child.

This is an ideal supplication when a couple decides to try for
a child. It is also an ideal prayer for those couples who cannot
bear a child for any medical reasons. ALLAH willing, the obstacle
of bearing a child would be removed. The *du'a* ends with an
emphasis that ALLAH is *indeed Hearer of prayer.* Do we need any
other kind of reassurance?

*...And do not forget benevolence
between yourselves (spouses)...*

(Al-Baqarah 2:237)

For offspring

رَبِّ لَا تَذَرْنِي فَرْدًا وَّأَنْتَ خَيْرُ الْوَٰرِثِينَ ۞

Rabbi lâ tadharnî fardan wa anta khayru-l wârithîn.

My RABB! do not leave me alone, and You are the Best of the inheritors. (Al-Anbiya 21:89)

On several occasions, the Qur'ân cites the example of Zakariyya[PBH] and the birth of Yahya[PBH]. Zakariyya[PBH] was a nabi, and his wife was a virtuous woman. Although physical odds were against them, Almighty ALLAH had fulfilled their desires. ALLAH had cured the wife's barrenness and they were blessed with the birth of Yahya[PBH], who grew up to be a noble and chaste man. All three of them had exceptional qualities, and the Qur'ân describes: *"... they used to compete with one another in good deeds, and call upon Us with hope and fear; and they were humble before Us"* (*Al-Anbiya* 21:90).

As with the prayer in the previous page, this prayer is also ideal to seek to ALLAH for an able inheritor. All childless couples as well as those who wish to have more children should invoke ALLAH with this *du'a*.

*...if He desires you a good, there is
no repeller of His grace...*

(Yunus 10:107)

For offspring

رَبَّنَاوَاجْعَلْنَامُسْلِمَيْنِ لَكَ وَ مِن ذُرِّيَّتِنَآ أُمَّةً مُّسْلِمَةً لَّكَ وَأَرِنَامَنَاسِكَنَا
وَتُبْ عَلَيْنَا إِنَّكَ أَنتَ التَّوَّابُ الرَّحِيمُ ۞

Rabbanâ wa-j'alnâ muslimayni laka wa min dhurriyyatinâ ummatan muslimatan lak, wa arinâ manâsikanâ wa tub 'alaynâ; innaka anta-t tawwâbu-r rahîm.

Our RABB! and make us both Muslims to You, and from our offspring a nation Muslims to You, and show us our ways of dedication, and turn towards us. You indeed, You are the oft-Returning, most Rewarding. (Al-Baqarah 2:128)

Ibrahim^{PBH} and Ismail^{PBH} invoked this supplication while reconstructing the Holy House of Ka'bah.

This supplication is to be made by all the parents who wish to have their children lead an Islamic life, away from evils and *shirk*. What could be more saddening than to find our children deviating away from the Truth even though we practiced reverence? If ALLAH shows our children and us the right path, and we walk on it practicing *Taqwa*, then may be ALLAH will turn towards us in kindness. Surely, He returns with mercy and rewards.

This is an ideal prayer to be invoked daily, particularly by the parents who are raising their children in the challenging atmosphere of the West. As emphasized in this *du'a*, ALLAH will turn often with rewards to show us and our children ways of dedication.

Certainly We have created Man in the finest make.

(At-Tin 95:4)

For offspring

رَبِّ اِنِّى وَهَنَ الْعَظْمُ مِنِّى وَاشْتَعَلَ الرَّأْسُ شَيْبًا وَلَمْ اَكُنْ بِدُعَائِكَ رَبِّ شَقِيًّا ۞ وَاِنِّى خِفْتُ الْمَوَالِىَ مِنْ وَّرَآءِى وَكَانَتِ امْرَاَتِى عَاقِرًا فَهَبْ لِى مِنْ لَّدُنْكَ وَلِيًّا ۞

Rabbi innî wahana-l 'a<u>z</u>mu minnî wa-<u>sh</u>ta'ala-r ra'su <u>sh</u>ayba<u>n</u> wa lam akun bi-du'âi'ka rabbi <u>sh</u>aqiyya. Wa innî <u>kh</u>iftu-l mawâliya min warâi' wa kânati-mraa'tî 'âqira<u>n</u> fa-hab lî min ladunka waliyyâ.

My RABB! surely the bones in me are weakened, and the head flares with hoariness, and my RABB! never I have been unsuccessful in my prayers to you. And surely I fear my relations after me, and my wife is barren, therefore grant me from Yourself a trustee. (Mar-yam 19:4-5)

As a prelude to the history of Mar-yam^{PBH} and birth of 'Isa^{PBH}, the extraordinary incident with Prophet Zakariyya^{PBH} was mentioned. Zakariyya^{PBH} had made this supplication for a child. There were two impediments with Zakariyya^{PBH}—he was an old man and his wife was barren. To a casual observer, these debilities are impossible to overcome. However, we must remember that ALLAH is most Gracious and Hearer of prayer. Zakariyya's^{PBH} desire to have a child was not just for happiness of a family, but to have a trustee who would continue the responsibilities of his father in propagating the Truth. In response to this supplication, ALLAH not only rewarded Zakariyya^{PBH} with a child, but even named this child as Yahya^{PBH}.

This is an ideal prayer for a couple who are trying to get a child born to them. If they know that the wife has some kind of medical impediment, this ideal prayer must be invoked so that ALLAH willing, the medical problems would be removed.

...ALLAH creates what He pleases...

(An-Nur 24:45)

For offspring

رَبَّنَا هَبْ لَنَا مِنْ أَزْوَاجِنَا وَذُرِّيَّتِنَا قُرَّةَ أَعْيُنٍ وَّاجْعَلْنَا لِلْمُتَّقِينَ اِمَامًا ۞

Rabbanâ hab lanâ min azwâjinâ wa dhurriyyâtinâ qurrata a'yunin wa-j'al-nâ li-l muttaqîna imâmâ.

Our RABB! grant us out of our wives and our offspring the joy of eyes, and make us leaders of the reverent. (Al-Furqan 25:74)

True success of our lives would be if we could reach the Paradise by being reverent, and being patient in difficult times. We will be even more successful if our children and spouses can accomplish similar goals.

This supplication was made by such believers who devoted to the Truth, and did not turn deaf or blind to the Message of the RABB. They wanted the message of the Truth to propagate for generations through their children. This would be the joy of eyes to witness a glorious future. These Muslims were so convinced of the Truth that, to them, just practicing the reverence was not enough; they would like to lead others into the fold of Truth.

The next verse (*Al-Furqan* 25:75) confirmed that such believers would be rewarded with high places, as they were patient through all kinds of difficulty. They might have lost their earthly homes as unbelievers drove them away. As an ultimate reward, these believers would be greeted with salutation in their new homes at *high places*, which would be *excellent for rest and residence.*

...ALLAH has placed therein (—your wives) a lot of good.

(An-Nisa' 4:19)

For offspring

لَئِنْ اٰتَيْتَنَاصَالِحًا لَّنَكُوْنَنَّ مِنَ الشَّٰكِرِيْنَ ۞

Lai'n âtaytanâ sâlihan la-nakûnanna mina-sh
shâkirîn.

If You give us a good one, we shall surely be of the thankful ones!
(Al-A'raf 7:189)

As a prelude to this supplication, ALLAH has described the
process of evolution and procreation. Those who have some
knowledge of biology, realize that it is humanly impossible to
initiate and complete the process of procreation without the
help of ALLAH. Most atheist scientists also concede that Nature
play the entire role. Hundred and thousands of babies who are
born everyday are truly miracles performed by ALLAH. For such
a miraculous thing to happen in our lives, we need the help
of ALLAH through a supplication like this. ALLAH instructs that
would-be-parents should make this supplication for the birth of
their child.

In the following verse (*Al-A'raf* 7:189), ALLAH reminds that
even though parents receive the blessing of a child, often they
become ungrateful. We should thus remember to pray to ALLAH
during both difficult and good times.

Our religion is based on firm covenant with ALLAH, and we
must not turn it into our convenience to call upon Him only
when we are in trouble.

...He grants to whom He pleases females,
and He grants to whom He pleases males.

(As-Shura 42:49)

For offspring

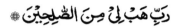

Rabbi hablî mina-s sâlihîn.

My RABB! grant me one of the doers of good. (As-Saffat 37:100)

In response to Prophet Ibrahim's[PBH] desire for a worthy child, ALLAH gave glad tidings of a son, Isma'il[PBH] (*As-Saffat* 37:101).

Subsequent verses described Isma'il's[PBH] good works—which included willingness to sacrifice himself for the sake of ALLAH. Ibrahim[PBH] did not ask for a male child, as many of us often do. Some of us feel that irrespective of gender just a healthy child is important. As we learn from this fine example of Ibrahim[PBH], we should rather ask for one who will do good actions. A baby will soon grow up. If our child does not turn out to be a good adult, then having a healthy baby or a male child is just a temporary pleasure.

This supplication is not only for a newborn baby; it can also be invoked to seek ALLAH's blessings on any child already born. The bundle of joy should remain joy to our eyes and to ALLAH (*Al-Furqan* 25:74) even when it grows up.

or He combines them males and females,
and He makes whom He pleases barren.
Surely He is all-Knowing, most Capable.

(As-Shura 42:50)

For offspring

رَبِّ إِنِّى نَذَرْتُ لَكَ مَا فِى بَطْنِى مُحَرَّرًا فَتَقَبَّلْ مِنِّى إِنَّكَ أَنتَ السَّمِيعُ الْعَلِيمُ ۞

Rabbi innî nadhartu laka mâ fî batnî muharraran fa-taqabbal minnî; innaka anta-s samî'u-l 'alîm .

My RABB! I do hereby dedicate to You what is within my womb to be devoted, so accept from me; surely You, only You, are the all-Hearing, the all-Knowing. (Al-i-'Imran 3:35)

Dedication of a coveted item to the RABB is the highest form of prayer. The Qur'ân refers Mar-yam's[PBH] mother simply as a woman, suggesting her insignificance, except some lineage to the family of 'Imran. As a person, she did not receive any special recognition in the Qur'ân. Yet, her devotion and sincere *du'a* was accepted. A dedication of the child in her womb to the RABB must not be misunderstood to be blood-sacrifice; it is the tireless effort in the right path that we all must exercise. When the baby girl was born, the mother was troubled as her expectation was for a male child. To the RABB, it is not the gender but the sincerity that matters. As the supplication qualifies, ALLAH is *surely all-Hearing, all-Knowing.* He knows very well everything in a womb (*Ar-Ra'd* 13:8), and in addition, what that child is going to do as it matures (*Al-i-'Imran* 3:36).

The baby girl grew up to be an example of purity, prompting Zakariyya[PBH] to long for such a pious child for him. She not only became the mother of a prophet, her virtues earned her the finest recognition—she is the only woman who is named in the Qur'ân. A Surah named after her, she is a Sign to the mankind (*Al-Anbiya'* 21:91, *Al-Mu'minun* 23:50). Mar-yam[PBH] and her son 'Isa[PBH] may be of the most famous people, yet they were the results of a sincere prayer from an insignificant expectant mother. Even if we are insignificant, ALLAH attentively listens to our every *du'a* and provides us beyond our imagination.

For a Sign

Rabbi-j'al lî âyat.

My Rabb! Provide for me a Sign! (Mar-yam 19:10)

Zakariyya^{PBH} was impressed with the devoutness of young Mar-yam^{PBH} as she was under his guardianship. He was childless and there seemed no practical hope for parenthood. He was old and his wife was barren. Yet, he asked ALLAH not to leave him without a child. The reason for getting the child was not amusement, but to carry forward the message of the RABB. The noble intention was accepted and ALLAH sent him a glad tiding of a child. It seemed puzzling that such physical disabilities could really be overcome. Zakariyya^{PBH} asked ALLAH to provide him with a sign that would indicate the glad tiding was indeed from his RABB. ALLAH instructed him to spend three days and three nights in meditation, without talking to anybody.

As Zakariyya^{PBH} contemplated on his RABB, he was reassured that ALLAH is indeed the most Powerful. The RABB who creates every thing in the world can also create a child for a seemingly incapable couple.

He it is Who shows you His Signs, and
sends down for you provisions from the sky...

(Al-Mu'min 40:13)

85

For knowledge

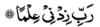

Rabbi zidnî 'ilmâ.
My RABB! increase me in knowledge. (Ta Ha 20:114)

ALLAH instructed Prophet Muhammad[PBUH] to invoke this prayer. The verse relates to an instruction not to hasten with the Qur'ân before it is completely revealed. As our RABB would increase the knowledge for our Rasul[PBUH], he would understand the newer verses as they continue to reveal.

For us, when our knowledge about the Qur'ân is limited, we should always make this supplication to better understand its message. The term *ilm* (lit. knowledge) is not restricted to religious knowledge alone. It covers knowledge in any field, be it technology, science, medicine, theology, etc. Only when we will have good knowledge in various disciplines, the understanding of the Qur'ân will be even easier.

We seek the knowledge from the best Teacher, who teaches the Qur'ân (*Ar-Rahman* 55:2). ALLAH is ever ready to teach us and inspire us only if we are attentive students. Since ALLAH explains the Qur'ân (*Hud* 11:1, *Al-Qiyamah* 75:19), and He is with us all the time, there can be no excuse of limited learning resources.

...Surely the knowledge is with ALLAH...

(Al-Mulk 67:26)

For knowledge

Rabbi hab lî ḥukman wa alhiqnî bis-sâliḥîn.

My RABB! grant me wisdom, and join me with the righteous. (As-Shu'ara 26:83)

History has repeatedly shown that preaching truth is hard and challenging work. This could be little easier if supported by wisdom.

Prophet Ibrahim^{PBH} was making *dawah* to his sire Azar and his community. The people were staunch disbelievers. Ibrahim^{PBH} while explaining to the people about the truth and reward of obeying ALLAH, invoked this supplication.

This supplication stresses that our knowledge should guide us to be righteous. By praying this supplication, we are eliminating the blind following of ancestral ways. Wisdom will enrich us to understand the Divine messages better, apply it into our lives, and in turn we could be righteous people.

*...whoever is granted wisdom, he is then
granted a great good indeed...*

(Al-Baqarah 2:269)

For knowledge

دَبِّ ٱشۡرَحۡ لِي صَدۡرِي ۝ وَيَسِّرۡ لِيٓ أَمۡرِي ۝ وَٱحۡلُلۡ عُقۡدَةً مِّن لِّسَانِي ۝ يَفۡقَهُواْ قَوۡلِي ۝

Rabbi-shrahlî sadrî. Wa yassirlî amrî. Wa-hlul 'uqdatan min lisâni. Yafqahū qawlî.

My RABB! expand for me my breast, and make my affair easy for me, and release the knot from my tongue, they may understand my speech. (Ta Ha 20:25-28)

A convincing argument, whether in written or spoken form, is based on lucid articulation created by strong knowledge.

Prophet Musa^{PBH} invoked this prayer while proceeding to the court of Pharaoh for the arguments. This supplication requests for increased knowledge base—an important requirement for arguments. There is additional request to remove physical limitations or limitation of resources, and lastly, to make lucid, easy to understand arguments. Although Musa's^{PBH} limitation was speech related, we are not just asking for the removal of same problem, but any problem that may hinder our quest for knowledge and its propagation.

As a reward of this *du'a*, Musa^{PBH} so successfully articulated his speech and arguments that many officials immediately rejected Pharaoh and embraced the truth.

Students, orators, speakers and writers should include this supplication in their daily prayers to ALLAH, so that their endeavors could become more fruitful.

AR-RAHMAN! He taught the Qur'ân.
He created Man; He taught him distinct speech.

(Ar-Rahman 55:1-4)

For sacrifice

إِنَّ صَلَاتِى وَنُسُكِى وَ مَحْيَاىَ وَمَمَاتِى لِلّٰهِ رَبِّ الْعٰلَمِينَ ۞ لَاشَرِيكَ لَهُ وَبِذٰلِكَ أُمِرْتُ وَأَنَا أَوَّلُ الْمُسْلِمِينَ ۞

Inna salâtî wa nusukî wa mahyâya wa mamâtî li-llâhi rabbi-l 'âlamîn. Lâ sharîka lahū; wa bi-dhâlika umirtu wa ana awwalu-l muslimîn.

Surely my Salat and my sacrifice and my living and my dying are for the sake of ALLAH - RABB of all the worlds. No partners has He; and thus I am commanded, and I am the foremost of the Muslims. (Al-An'am 6:162-163)

ALLAH taught ways of life and prayers to bring out the excellence in the Rasul[PBUH]. Our Prophet[PBUH] followed all the instruction to the word.

The doctrine of entire submission to ALLAH conveyed in Islam finds its manifestation in the life of Muhammad[PBUH]. His life, his every work, Salat, all kinds of sacrifices and even death is meant for ALLAH. Such is the concept of obedience to One and Only ALLAH. We should work, pray and do good deeds only to please our RABB. When we sacrifice our comforts, or even when we sacrifice an animal, we should do it because it pleases ALLAH. If we act to please humans only, this approach is close to committing *shirk*. In two verses, this supplication encompasses every aspect of our life.

As ALLAH has purchased our lives in exchange of the Garden (*At-Taubah* 9:111), we must lead our lives according to His wishes.

> *...your God is the One God,*
> *therefore to Him should you submit...*

(Al-Hajj 22:34)

For victory of Islam

رَبَّنَا افْتَحْ بَيْنَنَا وَبَيْنَ قَوْمِنَا بِالْحَقِّ وَأَنْتَ خَيْرُ الْفَاتِحِينَ ۞

Rabbanâ-ftaḥ baynanâ wa bayna qawminâ bi-l ḥaqqi
wa anta khayru-l fâtiḥîn.

*Our RABB! decide between us and between our people with the
Truth, for You are the Best of deciders.* (Al-A'raf 7:89)

Evil people always come up with crooked ideas. In the
township of Madyan in greater Syria, Shu'aib^{PBH} was preaching
the message of ALLAH. Like most other heedless communities,
the residents of Madyan also resisted to accept the Truth. Only
few people became Muslims. The elders warned Shu'aib^{PBH} that
they would drive him and his followers out of the township
unless these Muslims came back to their old way of living.
Shu'aib^{PBH} was not to come back as he was already rescued out
of the evil system. He knew that the best way was to rely on
ALLAH. Therefore, he invoked ALLAH to decide between the good
and bad based on the Truth.

Earnest prayers can help us resolve all controversies. Let us
rely on ALLAH for decision of truth over falsehood and let the
truth differentiate us, who are Muslims, from those who are
idolaters. We know that the righteous will definitely be amply
rewarded.

*...This day I have perfected for you your religion,
and completed upon you My blessing,
and have accepted for you ISLAM as the religion...*

(Al-Ma'idah 5:3)

For guarding loyalty

مَعَاذَاللّٰهِ إِنَّهُ رَبِّيَ أَحْسَنَ مَثْوَايَ إِنَّهُ لَا يُفْلِحُ الظَّالِمُونَ ۞

ma'ādha-llāhi innahū rabbî ahsana mathwāya. Innahū
lā yuflihu-z zālimūn.

*Refuge with ALLAH; surely He, my RABB, has made good my lodging.
Surely the wrongdoers are never made to prosper.* (Yusuf 12:23)

Yusuf's^{PBH} life is an example of contrast and irony. As he was
left in a well to die by his step-brothers, he was rescued by some
travelers. An Aziz intended to raise him as a slave or a son.
However, the wife of the Aziz desired Yusuf^{PBH} when he grew
up as an intelligent handsome man. How can Yusuf^{PBH} betray
the trust of a man who gave him a shelter in his home? Yusuf^{PBH}
not only obtained food and a roof over his head, but he was able
to expand his wisdom at the Aziz's house *(Yusuf 12:22)*.

Here we get a slight hint of Yusuf's^{PBH} future prosperity. He
had not directly asked ALLAH to provide him prosperity. He was
then just an abandoned brother, a slave picked up from a well and
exchanged for a paltry sum. The prosperity he mentioned might
not have been a suggestion for worldly riches, rather rewards in
the Hereafter. His knowledge, explanation of dreams and moral
integrity earned him recognition, high position, riches and also
reunion with his parents and brothers. Definitely, he received
his prosperity, both in this world as well as in the Hereafter.

*...Surely ALLAH does not love any
traitor, ungrateful ones.*

(Al-Hajj 22:38)

Hints for successful prayers

The prayers from the Qur'ân teach us ways to plead ALLAH. Although the prayers from the Qur'ân are the finest, we may also pray using our own words. Based on the principles of the prayers in the Qur'ân, certain points may be remembered about the prayers we invoke.

➤Do rely on ALLAH fully. He created the Universe, thus, relieving our distress is hardly a difficult issue. (pp. 5, 52)

➤Do glorify ALLAH in the prayers with appropriate qualifications. (pp. 11, 12, 13, 38, 53, 60, 62, 63, 66, 68, etc.)

➤Do ask for broad objectives—*give us good in this world, and good in the Hereafter*, instead of seeking temporary benefits. (p 9)

➤Do ask for good in the Hereafter. (pp 9, 10, 74)

➤Do offer gratitude for all the blessings that we receive. (pp 64, 65)

➤Do exert your own effort to overcome difficult situations. Success is not with the lazy or the withdrawn. (pp 30, 66, 67)

➤Do pray for and by yourself. ALLAH listens to every one, even to those who are apparently insignificant. (p 84)

➤Do pray for parents, children and for the *ummah*. (pp 18, 41, 60, 70, 74)

➤Do not expect instant results, although it may happen. (p 54)

➤Do exercise perseverance. All processes follow Natural Laws—the Laws of ALLAH. Your prayer may see the results in days, months or years later. You may not even live long enough to see the full result of some of your prayers. (pp 53, 54)

➤Do not be too specific about your request. We do not know if our desired object would really be good. Leave the final decision upon ALLAH. (pp 33, 54)

➤Do not ask for what violates ALLAH's Law. So, do not ask to make you a prophet or to bring back a dead person. (p 77).

➤Do not plead on behalf of evil people or for evil plans. (pp 58, 62).

Index

Names of Surah are in *italic*.

Abyssinia: 24
Accusation: 69, 70
Adam: 55
Al-Ahqaf: 64
Angel: 17, 22, 74
Al-An'am: 89
Al-Anbiya: 19, 29, 59, 78, 84
Al-Ankabut: 47
Al-A'raf: 10, 11, 43, 50, 55, 82, 90
Ark: 32, 66, 68
Arsh: 17, 22, 74
Ashraful Makhluqat: 5
'Asiya: 26
Al-'Asr: 75
Awakening, Day of: 38, 39
Ayyub: 29, 33
Azar: 52, 62, 87
Aziz: 34, 91

Bani Isra'il: 76
Al-Baqarah: 6, 9, 53, 56, 75, 79
Believers: 40, 41, 70
Birth: 64, 77, 78, 80, 81, 82, 83, 84
Brother: 11, 60
Bukhari, Sahih: 56

Canaan: 42
Cave dwellers: 7
Children: *see* Offspring

Dawud: 75
Death: 50, 51, 52, 89
Distress: 25, 29, 30, 31, 32
Ad-Dukhan: 31, 61

Earthquake: 10, 63
Eid: 72
Effort: 53
Egypt: 25, 51
Egyptian: 30, 46
Employment: 54

Faith: 37
Al-Falaq: 20
Al-Fath: 34
Al-Fatihah: 5
Faults: 31, 36
Fatimah: 26
Food: 72
Forgiveness: 55, 56, 57, 58, 59, 60, 61
Al-Furqan: 16, 81, 83

Garden: 6, 13, 26, 33, 38, 39, 74
Goliath: 75
Gomorrah: 45
Good in both worlds: 9, 10
Gratitude: 64, 65

Harun: 11, 25
Hasanah: 9, 10
Al-Hashr: 60
Hawariyyun: 37
Hellfire: 9, 14, 15, 16, 17
Al-Hijr: 5
Hud: 7, 58, 66, 86
Hudaibiyah: 34

Ibn Kathir: 9
Ibrahim: 8, 18, 39, 40, 52, 53, 62, 79, 83, 87
Ibrahim: 8, 18, 40
Immigration: 67
Al-i-'Imran: 9, 14, 15, 25, 33, 36, 38, 57, 73
Iraq: 49, 59
'Isa: 37, 72, 80, 84
Is-haq: 8
Ismail: 8, 53
Israel: 25, 71
Israelite: 30, 42, 46

Jalut: 75
Jeroboam: 71

Jethro: 54
Journey: 54, 66, 67, 68
Judgment, Day of: 15, 39, 40

Ka'bah: 53, 79
Al-Kahf: 7
Khadijah: 26
Knowledge: 86, 87, 88

Light: 61
Loyalty: 91
Lut: 45, 47

Madinah: 19, 24, 67
Madyan: 44, 54, 90
Al-Ma'idah: 6, 72
Makkah: 18, 19, 24, 67
Mar-yam: 26, 77, 80, 84, 85
Mar-yam: 80, 85
Mercy: 11, 12, 13
Mt. Sinai: 54
Muhammad: 19, 23, 24, 28, 36, 50, 67, 89
Al- Mu'min: 17, 22, 74
Al-Mu'minun: 12, 13, 23, 48, 68, 69, 84
Al-Mumtahanah: 52, 62
Musa: 10, 11, 25, 26, 30, 42, 44, 46, 50, 54, 63, 88
Muttaqi: 41

Al-Nahl: 9
Al-Naml: 65
An-Nas: 21
Natural calamity: 10, 48, 63
An-Nisa: 18, 24
Nuh: 32, 41, 49, 58, 66, 68, 69, 70
Nuh: 41, 49

Oppressors: 24, 25, 26
Offspring: 8, 77, 78, 79, 80, 81, 82, 83, 84

Parents: 40, 41, 64, 65, 76, 82
Perseverance: 50, 75
Pharaoh: 5, 25, 26, 30, 44, 50, 54, 88

Prayer, acceptance: 8
Prison: 34
Provisions: 71, 72, 73
Paradise: 41, 74
Punishment: 25, 32

Al-Qamar: 32, 69
Al-Qasas: 30, 46, 54
Al-Qiyamah: 7, 86
Qumran Valley: 7
Quraish: 23

Ar-Ra'd: 84
Ar-Rahman: 7, 86
Repentance: 31
Righteousness: 50, 51
Right path: 5, 6, 7

Sabr: 50, 75
Sacrifice: 89
Sad: 71
As-Saffat: 83
Safura: 54
Salat: 5, 8, 89
Shaitan: 21, 22, 23, 55, 74
Shelter: 54
Shirk: 18, 20, 89
Shu'aib: 54, 90
As-Shu'ara': 30, 39, 45, 69, 70, 87
Sickness: 29, 33
Sinners: 42, 43, 44, 45, 46, 47
Sodom: 45
Spider: 67
Sulaiman: 65, 71

Ta Ha: 86, 88
At-Tahrim: 26, 61
Talut: 75
Temptation: 34
Throne of Power: 17, 22, 74
Taqwa: 79
At-Taubah: 40, 52, 89
Taubah: 31
Tree: 54
Trial: 62
Truth: 6, 7, 19

Uhud, Battle of: 36

Victory: 19, 36, 90
Volcano: 45, 47

Al-Waqi'ah: 39
Wealth: 25, 29, 33, 91

Yahya: 77, 78
Yunus: 59
Yunus: 25, 44
Yusuf: 34, 51, 91
Yusuf: 34, 51, 91

Zakariyya: 77, 78, 80, 85, 84
Az-Zumar: 18

GUIDE FOR TRANSLITERATION

ا	Alif	a		ط	Tâ	t
ب	Bâ	b		ظ	Zâ	z
ت	Tâ	t		ع	'Ain	'
ث	Thâ	th		غ	Ghain	gh
ج	Jîm	j		ف	Fâ	f
ح	Hâ	h		ق	Qâf	q
خ	Khâ	kh		ك	Kâf	k
د	Dâl	d		ل	Lâm	l
ذ	Dhâl	dh		م	Mîm	m
ر	Râ	r		ن	Nûn	n
ز	Zâ	z		ه	Hâ	h
س	Sîn	s		و	Wâw	w
ش	Shîn	sh		ى	Yâ	y
ص	Sâd	s		ء	Hamzah	'
ض	Dâd	d				

Long vowels: â, î, û

Nun joined with next letter, and Tanwin: n

BIBLIOGRAPHY

1. Ali, Yusuf (1999) *The Meaning of The Holy Qur'an* (10th edn). Beltsville: Amana Publications.
2. Asad, Muhammad (1980) *The Message of the Qur'an* (1st edn). Gibraltar: Dar Al-Andalus.
3. Emerick, Yahya (2000) *What Islam is All About* (1st edn). New York: International Books & Tapes Supply.
4. Hassan, Masudul (1983) *The Digest of the Holy Quran* (1st edn). Lahore: Law Publishing Company.
5. Hoque, Zohurul (2000) *Translation and Commentary on the Holy Qur-an* (1st edn). Dayton: Holy Quran Publishing Project.
6. Kathir, Hafiz Ibn (2000) *Tafsir Ibn Kathir (Abridged)*. Houston: Dar-us-Salam.
7. Khan, Muhammad Muhsin (1994) *Summarized Sahih Al-Bukhari* (1st edn). Riyadh: Maktaba Dar-us-Salam.
8. Mir, Mustansir (2000) Irony in the Qur'an: A Study of the Story of Joseph. In *Literary Structures of Religious Meaning in the Qur'an* (ed. I. J. Boullata). Richmond, Surrey: Curzon Press.
9. Shah, Shahid N. (2000) The Alim. (Ver 6.0.11.1). Silver Spring: ISL Software Corporation.